Teaching
Young Children
With ADHD

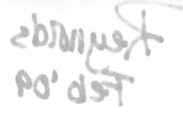

I give special dedication and remembrance to Mary Jo Thurston, Reading Specialist and Special Education teacher, whose love and dedication to children will be remembered by all who knew her.

—Richard A. Lougy

To Fred, the one who shares my life adventure, for all your love and undying support, and to Rachel and David for waiting patiently while I have dealt with the needs of other children. To my parents, Karl and Rose, who gave me everything I needed.

—Silvia L. DeRuvo

To Marci and Alex, with love and gratitude.

—David Rosenthal

Teaching
Young Children
With ADHD

Successful Strategies and
Practical Interventions for PreK–3

Richard A. Lougy ⚊ Silvia L. DeRuvo ⚊ David Rosenthal, MD

CORWIN PRESS
A SAGE Publications Company
Thousand Oaks, CA 91320

For information:

Corwin Press
A Sage Publications Company
2455 Teller Road
Thousand Oaks, California 91320
www.corwinpress.com

Sage Publications Ltd.
1 Oliver's Yard
55 City Road
London EC1Y 1SP
United Kingdom

Sage Publications India Pvt Ltd
B 1/I 1 Mohan Cooperative
    Industrial Area
Mathura Road, New Delhi 110 044
India

Sage Publications Asia-Pacific
    Pte Ltd
33 Pekin Street #02-01
Far East Square
Singapore 048763

Printed in the United States of America

Library of Congress Cataloging-in-Publication Data

Lougy, Richard A., 1944-
Teaching young children with ADHD : successful strategies and
practical interventions for preK-3 / Richard A. Lougy, Silvia L. DeRuvo,
and David Rosenthal.
       p. cm.
Includes bibliographical references and index.
ISBN-13: 978-1-4129-4159-4 (cloth)
ISBN-13: 978-1-4129-4160-0 (pbk.)
    1. Attention-deficit-disordered children—Education. 2. Attention-deficit hyperactivity disorder.
3. Early childhood education. I. DeRuvo, Silvia L. II. Rosenthal, David, 1958- III. Title.

LC4713.2.L68 2007
371.94—dc22

                              2006034838

This book is printed on acid-free paper.

07   08   09   10   11   10   9   8   7   6   5   4   3   2   1

Acquisitions Editor:	Stacy Wagner
Editorial Assistant:	Joanna Coelho
Production Editor:	Catherine M. Chilton
Copy Editor:	Julie Gwin
Typesetter:	C&M Digitals (P) Ltd.
Proofreader:	Doris Hus
Indexer:	Sheila Bodell
Cover Designer:	Monique Hahn
Graphic Designer:	Lisa Miller

Contents

Foreword

The arrival of this book on ADHD strategies for teachers of young children (ages 3–8) is very timely. Research points to the need for a range of strategies and services for preventing and addressing challenging behavior, including developmentally appropriate environments and teaching approaches that promote children's social-emotional and communication development. Social-emotional competence during the early childhood years is predictive of positive social and school outcomes in elementary school and beyond. There is mounting evidence that children exhibiting challenging behaviors are more likely to experience peer rejection and more punitive interactions with adults and to experience problems in school.

Besides acquiring a body of knowledge and skills, children must develop positive dispositions and attitudes. Social relationships are an important context for learning. Each child has strengths and interests that contribute to the overall functioning of the group. Children who exhibit behavior challenges often do not form good social skills, judgments, or emotional control. When children have opportunities to play together, work on projects in small groups, and talk with other children and adults in a safe and nurturing environment, their own development and learning are enhanced.

So often we receive requests from the field for help regarding behavior. We hire behavior specialists to give guidance, but there can never be enough support for the early childhood teacher. This book of strategies and information on ADHD for early childhood is a gift to the field. It holds many key components, taking into account the understanding of ADHD, social development, the educational environment, strategies that build on prior knowledge and connections, modeling (both peer and adult), positive adult relationships, and the importance of the parent.

Teachers will gain knowledge and skills through this clear, easy-to-navigate book. Our role as models for children should not be underestimated. Children thrive on the interest and attention we communicate to them. We should interpret children's disinterest, confusion, behavior, or lack of comprehension as signals that the approach we have been using is just not working. We must ask ourselves why we aren't reaching the child, instead of why the child isn't getting it. Many key questions are posed for teachers to use in examining their teaching style and methods. Young children are eager and enthusiastic learners trying to understand themselves and their world. Given the opportunity, children will naturally absorb new information, make connections, and acquire the skills needed for school success. The authors point out that positive, supportive relationships are essential not only for cognitive development but also for healthy social emotional development, and that such relationships have life-long implications. Recognition that individual variation is to be not only expected but valued requires that decisions about curriculum and adult interactions with children be as individualized as possible.

Family and culture play an important role in the lives of children. Being sensitive to the needs and preferences of families is critical. In the early years, the parent is the key to understanding the child. The parent is most familiar with the child's behavior, routine, and needs. Chapter 8 highlights the importance of the family as part of the intervention process. Strong partnerships between families and programs in which the unique strengths, concerns, and responsibilities of the family are fully recognized are necessary to the design and implementation of strategies and intervention to prevent and remediate challenging behavior. Parents are the key to the child. Opening the channels of communication with the parent helps in forming that important partnership for the child and in planning strategies. Forming relationships built on trust, respect, and empathy is one of the most important strategies for success.

The importance of accommodations and adaptations to the environment as intervention tools is discussed in detail. Successful accommodations, along with strategies to make the child feel safe and confident, are components of good teaching skills. Keeping the child the center of our practices supports good teaching for all. When these interventions and strategies are not effective in stemming challenging behaviors, further evaluation and assessment may be needed to add support for the child. There is an urgent need to identify children with challenging behaviors early in order to increase school success and decrease the escalation of more severe social and academic problems. Effective partnerships between early educators, families, and other team members can facilitate identification of the variables that trigger and maintain the challenging behavior and lead to the development and implementation of interventions that support the use of more appropriate behaviors.

This book gives the reader eyes to see children in new ways, courage to create innovative avenues of instruction, and tools with which to make a difference for young children with ADHD, their families, and teachers.

Meredith Cathcart, M.S.
Special Education Consultant
California Department of Education

Preface

With all that is available for classroom teachers on ADHD, one might legitimately question why we chose to write another book on this topic.

Through our research, we found that though there are many volumes written to help teachers of school-age children, not much has been written with the early childhood educator in mind. This unique book is specifically written for teachers of preschool and early school-age children. We wrote this book with the intention of *specifically* helping teachers who work with children from three to eight years of age. Even though you will read about academic and behavioral interventions that are specifically targeted for preschool and early school-age children, you will find that many of the interventions and recommendations can be applied to older, elementary school–age children as well.

This book will help teachers who face the intense time demands of working with children with attention-deficit/hyperactivity disorder (ADHD) as well as the challenges of addressing these children's educational needs with limited support. The reader will also find this book appealing because of the in-depth attention it gives to explaining learning difficulties that children with ADHD experience, as well as the presentation of practical classroom interventions.

One particular challenge for teachers is trying to meet the educational needs of children with ADHD without depriving the other children of classroom time and attention. The ideas shared in this book should make this challenge more manageable as the strategies discussed benefit the learning needs of all students.

As authors, our professional backgrounds offer the reader a wide range of experiences: therapeutic, educational, and medical. We draw on our many years of professional experiences to bring to the reader reasonable and effective interventions that can be used in a classroom. It is our belief that children with ADHD benefit most when families, teachers, and (when necessary) doctors work together. You will find in this book ideas and suggestions that support and guide readers through collaboration.

HOW THIS BOOK IS ORGANIZED

The book's chapters cover a range of topics. Chapters 1 and 2 present an overview of ADHD, outlining symptoms and etiology (that is, origins) of ADHD. When teachers better understand known causes for symptoms and can recognize that the traits seen in ADHD are just that—traits, and not acts of "willfulness"—they will find greater success when implementing this book's recommended interventions. In Chapter 2, we highlight two important topics: temperament and executive functioning. We felt temperament was important to discuss in light of the behaviors that young children typically bring to school and because we are often asked questions on the role of temperament in a young child's behaviors. We introduce to the reader the concept of "executive functions" because of increasing evidence of their important role in understanding the behavior of children with ADHD.

Chapters 3 through 6 cover social skills development, behavioral management, writing strategies for young students, academic and behavioral classroom accommodations, civil rights protections for ADHD children (Section 504 Plan), and changes in special education services (Individuals with Disabilities Education Act of 2004).

Chapter 7 explores answers to questions frequently asked about medication and the pros and cons of medicating very young children with ADHD. The chapter also offers a brief overview of alternative treatments for ADHD. Information is provided on possible side effects from ADHD medications that you may observe in a child on medication.

Chapter 8 discusses the importance and benefits of positive communication with parents and other caregivers. We offer specific ways to improve communication with these critically important people in children's lives by answering common questions such as "How do I tell the parents that I think their child may have ADHD?" and "Why didn't the parents tell me their child was on medication?"

The last chapter, Chapter 9, covers recommendations on self-care for teachers. No job is more satisfying than teaching children; however, no job in education is more demanding or stressful than being a classroom teacher. You will find in the appendices a list of Web sites on ADHD, vignettes giving an overview of ADHD case examples, developmental stages of ADHD, associated disorders found with ADHD, disorders and conditions that can mimic ADHD, as well as a list of books for teachers on ADHD.

THIS BOOK'S PURPOSE

The purpose of this book is not to discuss guidelines for diagnosing ADHD in young children. Rather the focus is to provide teachers with two critical tools:

- A better understanding of this disorder and how it impacts a child's educational and social/emotional development.
- Hands-on practical strategies that teachers can use in the classroom that will help them have a positive, lasting influence in the lives of the children that they teach.

An important first step for teachers in helping a young child with ADHD is to become familiar with the disorder so that they can recognize that problematic behaviors expressed by children with ADHD are not willful. Becoming familiar with behavioral and academic interventions will help minimize these behaviors and will prevent children with ADHD from being labeled "bad kids" and carrying that label throughout their educational careers.

This book will provide you, the early childhood educator, with hundreds of practical suggestions and interventions to help you minimize the effects of ADHD in your classroom and provide positive classroom outcomes for all of your students, but especially those with ADHD.

Acknowledgments

This book has taken the collective education, knowledge, and experience of its authors. This collaborative work would not have been possible without the support of our spouses, our children, and our colleagues. We also want to acknowledge the children we've worked with and their frustrating and often confusing behaviors that allowed us to practice our trades and become "experts" in the field. So, to them, the children with ADHD, we give our greatest thanks and compassion.

Corwin Press wishes to thank the following peer reviewers for their editorial insight and guidance:

Isaura Barrera
Associate Professor
University of New Mexico
Albuquerque, NM

Suzanne Beane, MA, NBCT
Pre-K Varying Exceptionalities Teacher
Cypress Elementary School
New Port Richey, FL

Carole Campbell
Early Childhood Specialist and Special Educator
University of Arizona South
Tucson, AZ

Michael Elium
Coordinator of Special Education Programs and Associate Professor
University of the Pacific
Stockton, CA

Sheri L. Green
Elementary Teacher
Muncie Community Schools
Muncie, IN

Karen J. Miller
Developmental-Behavioral Pediatrician
Associate Professor of Pediatrics
Tufts University School of Medicine
Boston, MA

Carol Reynolds
Principal
Frostproof Elementary
Frostproof, FL

Sandra F. Rief
Speaker, Author, Consultant
Educational Resource Specialists
San Diego, CA

About the Authors

Richard A. Lougy has been living and working in Sacramento, California, for the last 30 years, where he began his career as a middle school teacher. During that time, he also served as an elementary school counselor and later as a school psychologist. He currently oversees mental health services for Head Start and Early Head Start programs in a large metropolitan schooldistrict in Northern California. In addition, he has a private practice specializing in children with ADHD and related disorders. He has treated and worked with thousands of children with ADHD and their families throughout his career. In addition to coauthoring the book *ADHD: A Survival Guide for Parents and Teachers* (Hope Press, 2002), he has also written numerous articles on ADHD and regularly presents at state and national conferences. He lives in Lincoln, California, with his wife Linda.

Photo by Bill Mahon

Silvia L. DeRuvo, MA, is currently a Special Education Resources Development Specialist for WestEd Center for Prevention & Early Intervention, a nonprofit agency that works with schools, districts, state agencies, and national policymakers in the areas of educational research, products, and programs. Prior to her work at WestEd, Silvia was an elementary special educator for nearly 20 years, working with children with mild to moderate disabilities in integrated settings. She is also an instructor at Sacramento State University and speaks nationally on special education practices for the Institute for Educational Development.

Silvia holds a master's degree in communicative disorders, along with credentials in Multiple Subjects, Special Education Specialist and Resource Specialist Certification. She is the current past-president of CARS+ (The California Association of Resource Specialists and Special Educators).

She has published articles on special education policy issues, has contributed to *The Handbook of Goals and Objectives Related to California Content Standards,* and has authored or coauthored *Timesaving Strategies to More Efficiently Progress Monitor IEP Goals and Report Writing: Removing the Stress.* Silvia resides in Northern California with her husband and two children.

 **David Rosenthal**, MD, is a child, adolescent, and adult psychiatrist who earned his medical degree at the University of Iowa School of Medicine in 1986 and completed his residency in adult psychiatry and fellowship training in child psychiatry at the University of California, Davis, Medical Center. He practiced psychiatry in various settings in California for many years and treated thousands of patients with ADHD before co-authoring the book *ADHD: A Survival Guide for Parents and Teachers.* He has lectured widely on ADHD and mood disorders and is currently in private practice in Boulder, Colorado.

Yes, ADHD Is a Real Disorder!

1

MYTH OR FACT?

The goal of this book is to give teachers the necessary understanding and tools to work with children with attention-deficit/hyperactivity disorder (ADHD) in their classroom. An important beginning step for teachers is the acceptance of ADHD as a real disorder and not a myth, because preschool and school-age educational support is very important in minimizing problematic ADHD behaviors and learning challenges.

ADHD is not a mythical disorder recently fabricated by the American Psychiatric Association (APA) or pharmaceutical companies for personal gain, as suggested by some groups and writers. As Anastopoulos and Shelton (2001) note, "There is little justification for claiming that ADHD is merely a 'disorder of the 90's'" (p. 21). Descriptions of behaviors that are indicative of ADHD go back to the year 1902. The scientific community has researched the disorder for many years, both in the United States as well as in the international mental health community. Over the years, the diagnostic criteria have undergone numerous transformations, from changes in conceptual emphasis to changes in how the symptoms are listed. Despite the large body of literature on ADHD, the core neuropsychological impairments in ADHD have not been fully resolved (Doyle, 2006). The diagnosis of ADHD is still a fluid and dynamic process, and only time will tell whether the current criteria will hold up under future empirical scrutiny (Anastopoulos & Shelton, 2001).

DIAGNOSTIC CRITERIA

The name, definition, and diagnostic criteria for ADHD have changed a number of times over the last few decades, reflecting changes in the conceptualization of the disorder by experts in the field. These changes have led to confusion for practitioners, parents, and teachers. Developmental pediatricians, psychiatrists, psychotherapists, learning specialists, and many other experts all have their own unique and valid perspectives on what constitutes ADHD and how it should best be treated. Numerous research studies have contributed significantly to our understanding of this complex disorder, but much remains to be learned with respect to the most effective interventions for those with ADHD.

ADHD is currently recognized as a disorder with behavioral, emotional, educational, and cognitive aspects that are manifested to some degree in a child with ADHD every day of the year. The APA *Diagnostic and Statistical Manual of Mental Disorders* (2000) notes that "the essential feature of Attention Deficit Hyperactivity Disorder is a persistent pattern of inattention and/or hyperactivity-impulsivity that is more frequent and severe than is typically observed in individuals at a comparable level of development" (*DSM-IV-TR*, 2000, p. 85). The affected child will manifest persistent patterns of ADHD behaviors that are "more frequent and severe," unlike an unaffected child, who may show ADHD behaviors only at times. The APA manual also notes that

> signs of the disorder may be minimal or absent when the person is under very strict control, is in a novel setting, is engaged in especially interesting activities, is in a one-to-one situation . . . or while the person experiences frequent rewards for appropriate behavior. (*DSM-IV-TR*, 2000, pp. 86–87)

The context-related variability of the disorder, in which a child will manifest behaviors indicative of ADHD in one setting or time and not another, is often taken to mean that it isn't present (Anastopoulos & Shelton, 2001).

MANIFESTATIONS OF ADHD

ADHD is a disorder that is often misunderstood by teachers because there are many different manifestations of ADHD in children. Not all children present ADHD in the same way or to the same degree. The current diagnosis of ADHD is divided into four categories. The precise category that a child's diagnosis will fall under will depend on the component that is most representative of the child's behavior. The four subtypes are:

1. ADHD, Combined Type
    This diagnosis applies to a child who presents predominantly with inattention and hyperactivity, but not significant impulsivity (*DSM-IV-TR*, 2000).

2. ADHD, Predominantly Inattentive Type

This diagnosis applies to a child who presents with inattention, but neither hyperactivity nor impulsivity (*DSM-IV-TR*, 2000). This child is often seen as a daydreamer or as an underachiever, and is inattentive and unfocused. His or her distractibility is many times internalized and is not always recognized by teachers.

3. ADHD, Predominantly Hyperactive-Impulsive Type

This diagnosis applies to a child who presents hyperactivity and impulsivity that is maladaptive and inconsistent with his or her developmental level. The child does not usually present with inattention (*DSM-IV-TR*, 2000). This population of children typically has the most difficulties with schools and outside agencies (e.g., law enforcement or social services).

4. ADHD, Not Otherwise Specified (NOS)

This population, typically adolescents and adults, who don't meet the full criteria for ADHD but still present some of the symptoms, are often diagnosed with either ADHD-NOS, or with "ADHD in Partial Remission" (*DSM-IV-TR*, 2000).

The symptoms exhibited by children with these variations of ADHD, except for ADHD-NOS, will be covered in more depth in Chapter 2.

PREVALENCE OF ADHD

ADHD has been the most studied of all psychological disorders in children and is one of the most common reasons for referring children to psychiatric and mental health agencies (Barkley, 1990). For those seeking more information on this disorder, there are thousands of scientific articles, numerous books, support group newsletters, and Web sites available for your review. So much effort and study has been dedicated to ADHD because it has social and educational implications, and the cost to society for untreated ADHD is high. Children with ADHD usually have impairments across multiple settings—home, social interactions, and school (Barkley, 2000; DuPaul, McGoey, Eckert, & Van Brakle, 2001; Lavigne et al., 1996; Vaughan & Kratochvil, 2006). There is little debate that once ADHD has been diagnosed, the disorder persists throughout childhood in the majority of cases (Teeter, 1998). Early diagnosis and treatment are critical, therefore, for minimizing the problems affected children will encounter in academic activities and in interactions with peers and adults. Treatment of an affected child is most successful when all parties are involved: parent, school, and doctor.

ADHD is a disorder that affects 3% to 20% of the population, depending on the information source. Most experts accept a range of 3% to 7% as the percentage of the population diagnosed with ADHD (Vaughan & Kratochvil, 2006); however, one study suggested 4% to 12% as the range in an unscreened school-age population (6 to 12 years old; Brunk, 2000). Findings of studies conducted in New Zealand, Canada, and Germany show an overall prevalence rate of 3% to 7%, similar to prevalence rates in the United States (Hoagwood et al., 2000). Russell Barkley (1995), a recognized expert on ADHD, had proposed that more than 2 million school-age children have ADHD, and a more recent report from the 2003 National Survey of Children's Health stated that approximately 4.4 million children ages 4 to 17 years in the United States had a history of ADHD diagnosis (Bukstein, 2006).

Over the last three decades, the numbers have been increasing for children diagnosed with ADHD. According to the U.S. National Ambulatory Medical Care Survey, the number of children who received a diagnosis of ADHD increased 250% from 1990 to 1998. Kelleher, McInerny, and Gardner (2000) reported that pediatricians identified ADHD disorders in 9.2% of children in 1996, compared with 1.4% of children in 1979, an increase of 657%. Do these statistics represent an epidemic, a heightened awareness of the problem, or a variety of forces at work pushing the diagnosis?

We believe there are a variety of reasons for the increase in the number of children diagnosed with ADHD. First, there is a greater awareness by the general public about ADHD. Second, over the last decade, preschool and adolescent children are increasingly being identified with ADHD, whereas in the past, preschool children were rarely identified, and professionals felt that most children outgrew ADHD by the time they had reached adolescence. Today, we know that both age groups can be appropriately identified and diagnosed with ADHD. Third, because of insurance guidelines and restrictions, most children today are initially diagnosed with ADHD by pediatricians and family physicians. There are still very few *developmental* pediatricians. Often, referrals to mental health specialists (such as child and adolescent psychiatrists) are made only if a child is presenting significant mental health concerns in addition to ADHD. Unfortunately, the consequence can be that a child may be misdiagnosed either because of limited time for assessment or because of inadequate expertise in ADHD by a pediatrician or family practitioner. Although over-diagnosis does occur, the reality is that most teachers will have at least one child with ADHD in their classroom (Scahill & Schwab Stone, 2000).

RECOGNIZING AND UNDERSTANDING ADHD IN YOUNG CHILDREN

Diagnosing ADHD in very young children is very difficult. Very young children are expected to be inattentive, impulsive, and very active at times.

Anyone who has lived or worked with very young children understands that these kinds of behaviors can be the norm rather than the exception. Consequently, mental health and medical providers are usually very cautious when diagnosing a young child with ADHD.

The focus of this book is not to discuss guidelines for diagnosing ADHD in young children, but to provide teachers with a better understanding of this disorder and how it can impact a child's educational and social/emotional development. An important first step for teachers in helping a young child with ADHD is to become familiar with the disorder and to recognize that ADHD can present itself differently in children.

It is important also to note that even though a child may not meet the criteria for a diagnosis of ADHD, he or she can still present many symptoms of ADHD that will challenge him or her in a classroom or in social settings. Therefore, you will find the ideas discussed in the following chapters helpful in the management and education of many young children.

WHAT CAUSES ADHD?

According to the experts, ADHD is viewed as a neurobiological disorder with strong evidence of family genetic risk factors (Anastopoulos & Shelton, 2001; Barkley, 2000; Biederman et al., 1992; Comings, 2001).

Genetics

Heredity, or a positive family history, appears to be the most common identifiable cause of ADHD (Comings, 2001). In fact, the frequency of the disorder in siblings is much greater than in the general population. Studies of adopted children with ADHD found that ADHD occurred more often in the birthparents than in the foster parents (Barkley, 1995; Biederman et al., 1992; Comings, 2001). That these children develop the disorder despite being raised by unaffected adoptive parents suggests that the transmission is by genetic rather than environmental factors. Studies of twins suggest that ADHD is one of the most heritable of the psychiatric disorders (Biederman et al., 1992; Levy, Hay, McStephen, Wood, & Waldman, 1997).

When environment plays a role in the development of ADHD, environmental factors alone do not cause ADHD (Barkley, 1990). However, in populations with a genetic predisposition, early environmental insults (e.g., maternal smoking, obstetric complications) or other factors, such as maternal alcohol consumption, significant prematurity of birth, and smallness for gestational age, may increase or play a contributing role in the probability of developing ADHD in childhood over and above the risk determined by genetics alone (Barkley, 1997).

ADHD is seen today as primarily a *polygenic disorder* (meaning that more than one gene contributes to it) that can be minimized or exacerbated by environmental factors. Studies from recent years, for example, are finding specific genes that contribute to ADHD ("Current ADHD Insights," 2004).

Biological Contributors to ADHD

ADHD is a biologically determined spectrum disorder presenting a myriad of variables and distinctions, yet it is often best treated by making conscientious changes to the environment and through medication. ADHD can manifest itself in various ways in each individual, and consequently, no child should be thought of as a poster child for ADHD.

ADHD actually refers to several chronic and distinct neurobiological disorders that interfere with an individual's capacity to regulate age-appropriate activity level, inhibition, and attention; however, there is no one blood test, brain scan, or definitive psychological test that can currently diagnose ADHD. The lack of a definitive test is not unique to this disorder, but applies to most psychiatric disorders, including disorders such as schizophrenia and autism (National Institute of Mental Health, 1999).

Brain scans of children with ADHD—which, it should be noted, are done for research purposes only and are not recommended for the routine evaluation of children with ADHD—can demonstrate decreased metabolic activity in areas of the brain thought to be responsible for the regulation of attention and inhibition; however, no one specific area or subsystem of the brain causes ADHD by itself (Gustafsson, Thernlund, Ryding, Rosén, & Cederblad, 2000).

The variability in symptoms in individuals with ADHD can be explained in part by anomalies in different parts of the brain circuitry. Children with ADHD show decreased metabolic activity in cortical areas of the brain that are thought to be responsible for the regulation of inhibition and attention (Durston et al., 2003). Medications used to treat ADHD act on neurotransmitters, such as dopamine and norepinephrine, which are active in the basal-frontal circuitry. When Ritalin or other stimulant medications are administered, for example, previously underactive structures that are involved in moderating motor activity and distractibility become more aroused (Vaidya et al., 1998).

Nerve Cell

To understand the role of neurotransmitters in ADHD, it's helpful to understand the role of the nerve cell. The nerve cell is not only the holder of the neurotransmitters, but also the roadway on which messages pass through the central nervous system (see Figure 1.1).

Figure 1.1   Nerve Cell

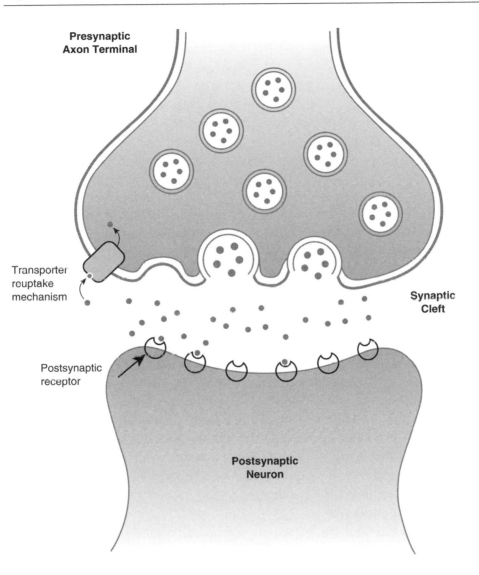

SOURCE: Reprinted with permission from *ADHD: A Survival Guide for Parents and Teachers*. Copyright ©
2002, Hope Press. Used with permission.

Communication within nerves is electrical, whereas communication
between nerves is chemical. An electrical impulse traveling through one nerve
(the presynaptic nerve) triggers the release of the nerve cell's
neurotransmitter from the cell into the *synaptic cleft*, or space between the
nerve cell's terminal end and adjacent nerve cells. These neurotransmitters
then bind to receptor sites on adjacent nerve cells, and electrical impulses are

generated in these nerves. In this way, information gets passed from one nerve cell to potentially millions of other cells in the central nervous system (Lougy & Rosenthal, 2002).

The movement of impulses across the synapse is the physiological mechanism by which we learn. Garber, Garber, and Spizman (1996) use the example of learning to play a piano. When we learn to play the piano, electrical impulses must make their way from the fingers to the brain and back again. With each practice, the pathway becomes better established and we play the piano more fluently. They state: "Learning occurs after an electrical impulse produced by a stimulus is transmitted and moves across a neuron-synaptic course several times" (Garber et al., 1996, p. 89). This explains why repetition is so important. With practice and repetition, the pathway becomes automatic. "If in ADHD these neural bridges are blocked or incomplete, whatever is being learned does not become automatic" (Garber et al., 1996, pp. 89–90).

Neurotransmitters

In recent years, many neurotransmitters' systems, each with their own specific brain circuits, have been identified in the brain, although the exact number has yet to be determined. Each system uses its own unique neurotransmitter to transmit messages within that system, although separate systems are able to communicate with each other.

The two primary neurotransmitter systems most directly involved in ADHD are the dopamine and norepinephrine systems. Dopamine and norepinephrine levels influence a variety of behaviors, including attention, inhibition, motor activity, and motivation, and relative deficiencies in these neurotransmitters help explain the signs and symptoms seen in those with ADHD. These two neurotransmitter systems work in concert with each other to control attention, inhibition, and motor planning. The medications used in the treatment of ADHD intervene by regulating norepinephrine and dopamine levels, thereby normalizing brain function and improving self-control (Barkley, 1990; Shekim, Javid, Dans, & Bylund, 1983).

Put somewhat differently, medications can stimulate a child's "brake pedal," thus providing support for some children whose feet are always on the "gas pedal" (Taylor, 1994).

CREATING AN OPTIMAL LEARNING ENVIRONMENT

Although ADHD has a strong biogenetic basis that is the primary factor in ADHD expression, environment can affect the adaptation and expression of these characteristics. The extent to which and manner in which "we can alter the environment may reduce the impact of symptoms of ADHD and the overall adjustment of individuals" (Teeter, 1998, p. 20).

Children with ADHD who are taught in a chaotic and highly stimulating classroom setting will often present more problems than a child taught in a more structured and calming setting. The classroom environment can accentuate or attenuate many of the traits of ADHD.

"Goodness of Fit" in Schools

Unsupported children with ADHD often are presented with many challenges in school, and statistics are not positive. One study reported that nearly 2% of 3- to 5-year-olds met the criteria for ADHD and found that problematic behavior ratings were two standard deviations greater than unaffected children. Also, pre-academic deficits in math and reading, as well as fine motor skills, were more frequent at the time of school entry with children diagnosed with ADHD (Vaughan & Kratochvil, 2006). Roughly a third of affected children will be held back one grade in school. About one-third will not complete high school, and between 40% and 50% will receive special education services. More than half have an oppositional component to their ADHD that gets them into trouble with school staff. Up to 15% to 20% will be suspended or expelled from school because of their behavior (Barkley, 1995).

These are not pleasant statistics. With more appropriate educational supports, children with ADHD can be more successful. Schools are currently struggling to find ways to appropriately teach the active child. Admittedly, the most patient of teachers can be easily worn down. The classroom experience can be even more difficult if there is a poor fit between teacher and child.

An important goal of this book is to provide teachers with suggestions to make attainable a "good fit" between them and children with ADHD. We recognize how difficult this can be. Traditional classroom settings may not provide enough flexibility to encourage stress-free circumstances for all kinds of children. Also, educational requirements and teacher preferences make some characteristics more acceptable than others. Success requires hard work by the teacher, knowledge about ADHD, and empathy for the child.

Teachers can, to some degree, modify their handling of children who are challenged by the symptoms of ADHD. Teaching styles can, at times, be adapted to the learning style of the child with ADHD, and classroom accommodations can sometimes be put in place to address the child's educational and behavioral challenges. However, it is important to recognize that in school there are limitations to the goodness of fit. Some of the behaviors of children with ADHD are so pronounced and problematic that even with significant accommodations, goodness of fit is nearly impossible to achieve.

SUMMARY

Our knowledge about ADHD has advanced greatly over the last decade, and as a result, affected children are achieving greater success. Children with ADHD are presented with a number of challenges in school and at home. Schools can go a long way in providing environmental changes to make the school day more positive for the affected child. Children with ADHD generally want to do the right thing but have great difficulty doing it. Core symptoms of ADHD (such as difficulty completing tasks, waiting one's turn, waiting in line, following directions, and self-regulating emotional outbursts) make day-to-day performance in school more difficult.

But the dilemma for many affected children is not that they are not ready for schools, but that schools are not ready for them. Toward better preparing schools and teachers for the children with ADHD who will inevitable be on their playgrounds and in their classrooms, this book offers a number of recommendations and interventions to make the teaching day more successful.

Recognizing ADHD   2

Primary Symptoms and Common Impairments

The primary symptoms associated with ADHD are inattention, hyperactivity, and impulsivity. The relative degree and pattern of these primary symptoms helps clinicians better index this disorder for diagnostic purposes. Not all children with ADHD, as noted in Chapter 1, will present these symptoms in the same way or to the same degree. ADHD probably represents the extreme end of a spectrum of normal human traits that we all possess, and, as with other human traits, ADHD undergoes developmental changes with maturity (Lougy & Rosenthal, 2002). This chapter will focus on inattention to a much greater degree than hyperactivity and impulsivity, as children who are inattentive tend to be overlooked far more than those displaying outwardly noticeable symptoms.

To be diagnosed with ADHD, "some impairment from the symptoms must be present in at least two settings (e.g., at home and at school or work) [and] there must be clear evidence of interference with developmentally appropriate social, academic, or occupational functioning" (*DSM-IV-TR*, 2000, p. 85). A young child, therefore, may present hyperactive behaviors in a preschool or school-age classroom, but not meet the level for a diagnosis of ADHD. His or her behavior must show significant impairment in two environmental settings, which means that the child must exhibit the hyperactive behavior at home as well as at school. If the behaviors are only seen in one setting, then the behavior is more likely a result of the environment rather than ADHD. A young child who is immature emotionally may find an unstructured classroom environment so stimulating that he or she cannot keep his or her emotions in check and have very active behavior. This same child may not have any of these behaviors when the environment is calm, structured, and controlled. In the same vein, the child with a cluttered home environment that lacks structure may have "wild" behavior at home, but respond positively with controlled behavior in a structure classroom setting. Therefore, we cannot always assume that a child who wiggles has ADHD.

We strongly recommend that you refer to Resource A in the back of this book, beginning on page 150. There you will find in-depth profiles of six children, spanning from preschool through third grade, who have been diagnosed with ADHD. These profiles demonstrate the variety of symptoms that children can present, various responses from parents and the medical community, and updates on the results of intervention and medication to date.

INATTENTION

It is important to note that it is not uncommon for preschool and early school-age children to be inattentive. In fact, it would be uncommon if a classroom teacher found the opposite to be true. In one report based on parent-teacher survey, 40% of four-year-olds displayed problems of inattention, yet the majority of these problems did not persist after three to six months. Also, in only 10% of those children showing inattention did the inattention result in academic or behavioral problems by the second grade. Thus, relatively few children who show early ADHD symptoms are significantly impaired or show significant ADHD symptoms in later grades. Last, because of a great deal of developmental variability among normal children with respect to behaviors that can mimic ADHD characteristics (including inattention, low frustration, noncompliance, and overactivity), professionals are looking for more reliable methods for assessing ADHD in very young children (Barkley, 1997; Teeter, 1998).

Notwithstanding these limitations and cautionary signs when diagnosing ADHD in young children, young children can still appropriately be diagnosed with ADHD (Barkley, 1990). Studies can vary as to age of onset, but in one study, about a third had an onset before three years of age, another third first showed symptoms before ages five or six years, and the remaining third first displayed their symptoms between six and seven years (McGee, Williams, & Freeman, 1992). In terms of psychosocial and academic impairments, one study suggested that the earlier the onset, the more likely the child will be challenged by associated disorders seen with ADHD (e.g., learning disabilities, anxiety, or defiant behaviors; McGee et al., 1992). However, the deficits were matters of degree and not of the kind in this study.

Much like the older child with ADHD, the preschool and early school-age child with ADHD often doesn't attend when given directions, sometimes leading to early referrals for evaluation of ADHD. The rise in preschool referrals for ADHD, in part, seems to be related to increased expectations placed on the child by preschool teachers or childcare staff who expect the child to comply with requests and to play cooperatively (Weiss & Hechtman, 1993).

Predominantly Inattentive

Children with ADHD who present with the predominantly inattentive subtype (ADHD-I) may sit and quietly zone out; they are internally rather than externally distracted. They often are seen as underactive, foggy, and cognitively sluggish. Younger children who have the predominantly inattentive subtype are unlikely to be referred for professional evaluation of ADHD because they do not display more commonly recognized disruptive behavior (Barkley, 1995; Layey et al., 1998). Early elementary children who do not manifest the hyperactive symptom may also be initially overlooked by the teacher, but they tend to have increased rates of academic problems as they advance in their schooling (Barkley, 1997).

Inattentive behaviors manifested by these children are, however, chronic, pervasive, and problematic in their day-to-day activities. These children have great difficulty attending to one thing because they often pay attention to everything! One child may constantly scan the environment around her, distracted by all things except what needs her attention. Lacking the selection control to dispose of worthless information, she can often hear the lights buzz and the clock tick, making it difficult to determine which sounds should receive attention (Levine, 2002). Internally distractible, she may even look as if she is paying attention, but instead is attending to the clothes the teacher is wearing, the glasses on the teacher's face, and the color of her teacher's eyes. As she sits in class, she is also aware of the seams of her clothes on her skin and the pressure of her shoes on her feet. With all of this information activating her sensory perceptions, she will have a difficult time attending to the important aspects of an instructional period. With so much calling for her attention, she will usually choose to attend to something that she finds immediately gratifying to help block out the other input that is calling for her attention.

Inattentive Behaviors Often Seen in Preschool and Early School-Age Classrooms

- Difficulty paying attention when given directions by the teacher
- Difficulty staying focused on a school task or play activity for an extended period of time compared with other children in the classroom
- Does not seem to be listening when spoken to or given directions
- Often does not complete school tasks and has difficulty with follow-through in the classroom

- Is often forgetful and fails to remember daily rules or activities
- Often will be inattentive during classroom discussions and needs constant reminders to "join the group"
- Plays alone and is often "in his or her own world"
- Frequently daydreams

Short "Interest" Span

When listening to teachers and parents, a common complaint is that their child does not listen to instructions, becomes easily bored, doesn't finish assigned tasks, and daydreams. These children have difficulty with sustained attention when asked to attend to routine and laborious tasks. They have a difficult time planning: planning involved in coming to the end product of a task, such as cleaning their room or finishing a multistep chore. They often lack age-appropriate organizational skills to help them sequence the steps needed to complete a task, often leaving them unable to even begin a project without outside support to help them. A typical child without ADHD can also be less attentive when involved in routine activities; however, these children generally find it easier to stay with the task to completion, even though they may find it boring to them.

A child with ADHD often doesn't attend when given directions, so he or she may make decisions based on partial information, leading to incomplete or forgotten work. This child may only attend to the first part of the directions, and in his impulsivity, begin the task before the directions are completed, or he may only be attending to the last part of the directions and may have missed the initial part of the instruction. In either case, he will not be able to complete the assignment as directed, and will be confused about what he has done wrong.

He is likely to have difficulty with focused and sustained attention when involved in laborious or routine activities that might occur during classroom seatwork or when tackling tedious homework (Barkley, 1990). Russell Barkley (1995) suggests that when parents, teachers, and professionals say that children with ADHD have a short attention span, what they really should say is that they have a "short interest span." However, when affected children are introduced to high-interest, novel situations, or when situations are varied and stimulating, children with ADHD can be as attentive as those children without ADHD (Frick & Lahey, 1991; Zentell & Dywer, 1988), or when the rates of reinforcement are optimal, frequent, and immediate (Douglas & Parry, 1994; Pfiffner & Barkley, 1990). These children baffle their parents and teachers by being able to attend for long periods of time to TV shows, video games, and other activities that are novel to them like classroom experiments or an engaging assembly. In fact, when involved in high-interest activities, they can be *hyper-focused*—so focused on what they are doing that they are oblivious to what is happening around them.

Inattention in Preschool

Children, by preschool age, generally have begun to employ strategies to help them remember to remember (Siegel, 1999); however, children with ADHD, due to developmental delays in prefrontal functions, are less successful at this important task. An important component of remembering is a factor called *attention*. Although research is still ongoing around attentional and memory problems in preschool-age children, research does suggest that preschool-age children with ADHD are less attentive on structured tasks and more impulsive than children without ADHD (Campbell, Pierce, March, Ewing, & Szumowski, 1994). They are less attentive and cooperative during group activities (Alessandri, 1992; McIntosh & Cole-Love, 1996). For many preschoolers with ADHD, development of the ability to shift from resolving disputes with behavior to settling disputes with words is delayed (Campbell, 2002; Campbell et al., 1994). Additional delays in terms of attention and memory may also negatively affect children's readiness for school both academically and socially because of their problem behaviors (Campbell, 2002).

Motor control and persistence during tasks that require working memory are typical stumbling blocks for affected preschoolers (Mariani & Barkley, 1997). Because preschoolers with ADHD often have difficulty sitting still while looking at a book or patiently trying to manipulate a crayon, many children with ADHD seem immature and do not do well in preschool or kindergarten settings (Anastopoulos & Shelton, 2001).

Inattention and Play

Attentional differences in play are most prominent during "structured play" versus "free play." Children with ADHD can be indistinguishable from other preschool children during free-play activities, but are significantly different during structured play when compared to their typical peers. In structured-play activities such as table work, they leave their seats more often and tend to be more aggressive, demonstrating behaviors such as hitting, biting, throwing things, and kicking (Teeter, 1998).

Inattention in Early Elementary Classrooms

When children enter kindergarten or early elementary grades, they are challenged with a variety of new tasks that require self-regulation (Levine, 1987). Children with ADHD have pronounced difficulty in meeting these challenges. In the classroom, they have trouble attending to teacher directions. They have difficulty completing worksheets or classroom assignments because of daydreaming, and they are distracted by movements in the classroom. Young children with ADHD often have difficulty remembering to take notes home from the teacher. They can become distracted and not turn in assigned work, and they often will lose or misplace important items from their "messy" desk or backpack.

Although inattentiveness is more likely to occur during completion of chores or class assignments, it also can occur during play. The child with ADHD will shift from one toy to another, leaving a trail of discarded toys on the floor. Inattentiveness can also be seen in board games, where the child can become quickly bored and does not want to continue to play until the end of the game.

The word *attention* may actually refer to a number of different concepts or subtypes, all lumped together into a single word. Interruption in any one or in all of these subtypes can interfere with day-to-day functioning in school or at home, and this is a fundamental problem in children with ADHD. Sam and Michael Goldstein (1998) divide attention into the following five subtypes:

1. *Divided attention:* A child having difficulty taking notes and paying attention to the teacher simultaneously would be considered to have a problem with divided attention: the inability to complete two tasks simultaneously.

2. *Focused attention:* A child who is described as a daydreamer, who is preoccupied with other activities instead of what is being talked about, and who has an inability to attend to the task at hand, would be considered to have a problem with focused attention.

3. *Selective attention:* A child who is distracted by outside noises or who has an inability to ignore competing or irrelevant stimuli, such as a door closing or a child walking down the aisle to the front of the room, would be considered to have a problem with selective attention.

4. *Sustained attention:* A child unable to remain on a task long enough to sufficiently complete that task, or who has an inability to maintain attention when completing a task, would be considered to have a problem with sustained attention.

5. *Vigilance and readiness to respond:* A child who is unable to wait for the next spelling word to be presented by the teacher, or a child who has difficulty with listening, attending, and getting ready to respond, would be considered to have a problem with vigilance and readiness to respond.

A child with ADHD is challenged by all, if not most, of these subtypes.

Effects of the Inability to Self-Regulate Attention

Difficulty in self-regulating attention often has two pronounced and serious effects: variability in task performance and gaps in learning.

Variability in Task Performance

A primary pattern of behavior observed in children with ADHD is variability in task performance. Inconsistent task performance often leads to misunderstanding by teachers and caretakers: "He remembered to turn in his math paper on time yesterday; why can't he remember today?" Barkley (1990) contends that this variability in performance is particularly useful in diagnosing ADHD. Unfortunately, this erratic performance is confusing to the affected child, his or her teachers, and his or her parents. The ability to perform on some days and not on others brings a heavy toll of unfair accusations of laziness and willfulness (Levine, 2002; Levine, Busch, & Aufesser, 1982).

Gaps in Learning

One primary concern around self-regulating attention is that a young child with this problem can develop gaps in learning. Important information introduced by a teacher is not heard or remembered because of difficulties with maintaining attention. This can become especially important as the child advances in grades. One study found that students with ADHD–Predominantly Inattentive Type (ADHD-I) are at risk for arithmetic calculation difficulties. Their diminished attention capacity (especially selective attention) may impair their ability to focus on and master basic math facts during the primary grades (Marshall, Schafer, O'Donnell, Elliot, & Hardwick, 1999). Of the various learning problems that can occur in the ADHD population, reading disorders occur most often (August & Garfunkel, 1990). Levine (2002) notes that academic breakdowns occur in the six following areas for children with ADHD and learning problems:

1. Trouble mastering skills

2. Trouble acquiring facts or knowledge

3. Trouble accomplishing output

4. Trouble understanding

5. Trouble approaching tasks systematically

6. Trouble with the rate and amount of demands

ADHD and other associated learning problems create a very difficult classroom experience for most of these children. Strategies to support classroom instruction for these children are discussed at length in Chapters 5 and 6.

Difficulties With Adults Due to Inattention

Unfortunately, young children, because of difficulties with attention, can experience negative interactions at a very young age with adults. Ongoing battles around getting a child to remember to flush the toilet, line up at recess, or "listen when I am talking," can cause a young child to develop feelings of victimization and low self-esteem.

Often these behaviors are symptomatic of ADHD and not "willful behavior." Many times, inattention and impulsivity render children with ADHD unable to consistently follow rules or comply with requests. Consequently, children with ADHD often need, especially when involved with tedious tasks, high repetition to demonstrate their knowledge of the task and to increase the chances that the positive behaviors will become more automatic. If caretakers and school staff are not attentive to these cognitive and processing differences seen in an ADHD child, the child will be at higher risk for developing other problematic behaviors and secondary disorders (e.g., mood or oppositional defiant disorders [ODD]).

HYPERACTIVITY

Hyperactivity is not just high level of activity, but disorganized and purposeless activity. Hyperactivity refers to a range of excessive body movements ranging from restless, incessant fidgeting while seated to frantic running around the room for no apparent reason. The hyperactive child is often referred to as "always on the go" and "driven by a motor" (*DSM-IV-TR*, 2000). He jumps, wiggles, squirms, runs, and hardly sits still or walks calmly from one place to another. He pokes, grabs, and touches things, especially things he shouldn't. He has difficulty playing or engaging in leisure activities quietly and is accident prone. He can talk excessively, hang on the edge of a chair, or make excessive noises during quiet times. He is constantly loud and noisy when playing, whistling, clicking, making sounds, and producing an endless stream of chatter. In a nutshell, he has great difficulty managing his activity level and is seemingly unable to stop without constant reminders or interventions.

An affected child's incessant motor activity and restlessness is especially troublesome when the child reaches preschool or school age. Staying seated on the school bus or in class can be especially challenging. A child may have difficulty walking in line or staying seated at her desk. Even when staying seated, she can continue to be hyperactive, but in different forms, such as noisily tapping on a table or desk, rocking the desk chair, or swinging her feet to and fro. In preschool, an affected child has difficulty sitting in one place for circle time, lying down on a mat for the duration of rest time, or refraining from running when asked to line up.

Children in a classroom are asked to sit quietly at their desks, follow the teacher's directions, not bother the children next to them, and not fidget or rattle things while working. It would be easier for some of these hyperactive children to lie on a bed of nails than to master these behaviors!

Hyperactive Behaviors Often Seen in Preschool and Early School-Age Classrooms

- Often fidgets with hands or feet or squirms in seat or falls out of seat
- Often leaves seat (or circle time activity) during lesson when remaining seated is expected
- Often runs about or climbs excessively in situations where it is inappropriate
- Has difficulty playing or engaging in leisure activities quietly
- Often talks excessively or makes noises
- Often is "on the go" or often acts as if "driven by a motor" (*DSM-IV-TR*, 2000)
- Often tosses toys or other objects

In very young children, hyperactivity and impulsivity are the two ADHD symptoms most pronounced and noticed by teaching staff.

IMPULSIVITY

Impulsivity, or failure of inhibition, coupled with inattention, appear to be the primary and the most serious and sustained symptoms of ADHD in children and adults (Barkley, 1990). Unlike hyperactivity, which often diminishes with age, both cognitive impulsivity and inattention often continue into adulthood (Weiss & Hechtman, 1993). Adults with ADHD often have difficulty inhibiting the impulse to say or do what pops into their minds without first measuring the consequences of their actions (e.g., calling the boss a "jerk" or leaving a job site without first clearing it with their supervisor). Such actions often lead to getting fired. Impulsivity is manifested by difficulty waiting one's turn, blurting out before thinking, and interrupting or intruding on others' time and space.

A child's poor impulse control often alienates others. Typically developing children may view a peer with ADHD as demanding, inflexible, or selfish.

They will not likely be understanding of or patient with another child who demonstrates impulsive behaviors such as taking things without asking, cutting in line, and playing before his or her turn in a game due to impatience. As a result, children with ADHD may be seen playing alone and are seldom invited to parties, asked to participate in recess games, or included in group activities in the classroom. Teachers experience frustration with impulsive children because they tend to begin tests before being given permission to start and often call out answers to questions without raising a hand (or raise a hand but then don't say anything when called on).

Impulsive Behaviors Often Seen in Preschool and Early School-Age Classrooms

- Blurts out answers before questions have been completed
- Has difficulty waiting his or her turn
- Interrupts or intrudes on others (violates space or boundaries) (*DSM-IV-TR*, 2000)
- Cannot wait for the teacher to call his or her name or pay attention to him or her
- Needs constant reinforcement and has difficulty with delayed gratification
- Will make many errors on an assignment in an effort to finish quickly
- Will begin assignments without waiting for directions
- Difficulty tempering unhappy feelings (e.g., inappropriate language, yelling, throwing things)

In summary, the preschool and early school grades are where children begin to learn ways to work out problems, fears, social roles, and the expectations and rules of family and society. A young child's successful mastery of these skills often assures enhanced self-esteem, social knowledge, and self-control. Children with ADHD often show developmental delays in mastering these important social-emotional skills because of developmental delays in attention, hyperactivity, and impulsivity.

OTHER BEHAVIORS OFTEN SEEN IN CHILDREN WITH ADHD

Noncompliant and Oppositional Behaviors (ODD)

Children with ADHD—especially those with strong hyperactive-impulsive behaviors—can often exhibit noncompliant and oppositional behaviors. The noncompliant and oppositional child with ADHD can be negativistic, hostile, and defiant toward peers and authority figures. He is commonly argumentative with adults, frequently loses his temper, swears, is often angry or resentful, and is easily annoyed by others. Sometimes oppositional and noncompliant behaviors in children will mask or suggest a mood disorder. Mood and oppositional disorders are discussed in more depth in Resource B.

Risk-Taking Behaviors

Children with ADHD often crave high-stimulus situations, which puts them at risk for accidents. This can be seen in the reckless behavior of an eight-year-old who decides to climb to the top of a tree, or a four-year-old who repeatedly runs downstairs after repeated warnings not to run. The urge to experience risk, the desire for that adrenaline high, is more common in these children than in most others the authors professionally evaluate.

It should be noted that children with ADHD don't always learn from their mistakes and will repeat risky behaviors more often than typical children do. They also seem to have a higher tolerance for pain than typical children, which may explain, in part, their poor choices around risky behaviors. Last, because of high impulsivity, they often will not take time to measure the consequences of their acts and consequently, are accident prone (Quinn, 1997). They are driven by the moment. Lavoie (2005) calls these children, who can frequently be found in hospital emergency rooms, the "ready, aim, fire kids."

Emotionally Volatile Behaviors

Children with ADHD can be emotionally volatile, experiencing unpredictable moods that go up and down in a heartbeat. They seem to wear their feelings on their sleeves, showing little restraint and little ability to control their emotions, which are often expressed in extreme and raw ways. Such feelings can overwhelm and sometimes frighten those around them. Other characteristics are low tolerance for frustration, irritability, quickness to upset, and vicious reactions to others who are irritating. These children cannot tolerate being teased. They tend to explode, but then appear happy a few moments later and genuinely surprised that others won't play with them.

Self-Centeredness

While self-centered behavior is common in preschool children, ADHD children, by contrast, can be especially self-centered, lacking awareness of their impact on others. Because they often don't believe that they are personally at fault when something goes wrong, they are quick to blame others for their own anger because they don't see the connections between their behaviors and the subsequent consequences. They don't see that their actions are connected to how others respond. Their own needs and wants seem to be their dominant concern. They want rules changed to satisfy their wants, and often demonstrate an "I don't care" attitude if confronted for their selfishness.

IMPAIRMENTS IN EXECUTIVE FUNCTIONING

Russell Barkley, a recognized international authority on ADHD, contends that a deficit in behavioral inhibition leads to impairment in four major areas of executive functioning. Impairment in executive functioning leads to the cognitive, behavioral, and social deficits seen in the ADHD population (Barkley, 1997).

The term *executive functions* refers to an individual's self-directed actions that are used to help that person regulate his or her behavior, that is, actions a person performs that help him or her exert more self-control and better reach his or her goals. It is, in some ways, a cognitive process that serves as a kind of supervisor or scheduler that helps one select strategies and integrate information from different sources.

Components of Executive Function

Barkley's (1997) model suggests six components of executive function. The first component is *behavioral inhibition*—the foundation on which the four other executive functions (listed in the following) are dependent. Barkley considers the following four executive functions to be covert, self-directed forms of behavior that yield information that is internally represented and exerts a controlling influence over the sixth component of the model—the *motor control and execution* system. Barkley suggests that in the ADHD population, these functions are impaired. The four executive functions dependent on behavioral inhibition are:

1. *nonverbal working memory* (holding events in mind, sense of time and imagination, hindsight and forethought—helps us guide behavior across time toward a goal)

2. *internalization of speech* (verbal working memory, means for an individual to describe or reflect on an event before responding to it, central to development of rule-governed behavior, which makes possible functions such as reading, comprehension, and moral reasoning)

3. *self-regulation of affect, motivation, and arousal* (not reacting purely on emotion, but evaluating events rationally, then reacting)

4. *reconstitution* (analysis, goal-directed behavior, flexibility, and promotion of problem-solving abilities and creativity)

The executive functions represent the internalization of behavior that helps us anticipate changes in the environment and events that lie ahead in time. Barkley (1997) sees behavioral inhibition as the lead function in the chain of events provided by the executive functions. Without proper functioning in behavioral inhibition, the executive functions cannot occur without interference.

If you know that keeping your favorite candy or chocolate nearby may be too tempting, you will put it away so it's not as readily available. A typical child knows if she has an exam the next day, she will put off watching her favorite TV program to study. On the other hand, a child with ADHD is often driven by immediate gratification and will watch the TV program, test or no test; she does not take time to measure the long-term consequences of her choice. Many children with ADHD show an aversion to delay, showing preferences for small and more immediate rewards compared to larger, delayed rewards (Doyle, 2006). An unaffected child understands the need to reach the long-term goal of getting a good grade, which becomes more important than the immediate gratification of watching a favorite TV program. These examples illustrate a normal developmental cognitive process utilizing self-control that is often missing in children with ADHD.

Behavioral inhibition, along with the four executive functions, exerts a controlling influence over the sixth component of Barkley's model, the motor control and execution system.

Studies measuring fine motor coordination, such as balance, pencil-and-paper mazes, and fine motor gestures, often find children with ADHD to be less coordinated in these areas (Mariani & Barkley, 1997). Simple motor speed tasks, such as measured by the finger-tapping rate test, is not as affected in ADHD children as are more complex motor movements in which motor sequences must be performed. Handwriting, for example, is an example in which flexibility and fluency of fine motor movement are built on complex arrangements of letters, words, and sentences. Speech is another example in which assembly of complex fine motor sequences is important to articulate language. ADHD children are more likely than unaffected children to have speech problems (Barkley, 1997).

It should be noted, however, that when assessing executive functions in preschool children, there is general debate about whether preschoolers do in fact display specific deficits in executive functioning. One reason for the debate is that in very young children, executive functions may be inadequately developed. However, differences in executive functions become more apparent with increasing age. Even though it is apparent that very young children can have substantial ADHD symptoms, it's possible that the executive model may not be applicable to this young age group ("Current ADHD Insights," 2004). Also, there have been minimal studies looking at executive functioning in preschool population (Doyle, 2006). Many of the interventions and recommended accommodations for ADHD children presented in the book, however, stem in part from Barkley's research. Adaptations for preschools, in particular, are pointed out when relevant.

TEMPERAMENT AND ADHD

Temperament is often mentioned as an alternative explanation to understanding ADHD behaviors in young children. In light of the fact that temperament can be an early risk factor for ADHD (Barkley, 1995), we feel that it is important, therefore, to discuss it in light of the fact that researchers on temperament suggest that many children diagnosed with ADHD do not have a disorder, but rather present with challenges because of a poor fit between their temperament and the environment. In addition to a poor fit, two other sources influence a child's adaptability: "noxious environments" (e.g., family dysfunction, neighborhood violence, poor schools) and "intrinsic problems" (e.g., learning disabilities, autism; Carey & McDevitt, 1995, p. 2).

Although there seems to be "no universal agreement on the definition of temperament at this time," the general usage of temperament "refers to an individual's behavioral style—the characteristic way he or she experiences and reacts to the environment" (Carey & McDevitt, 1995, pp. 10–11). A child's temperament influences how a child performs a task, such as a five-year-old learning to tie his shoes. Will the child do it rapidly with a frown on his face, perform it slowly, singing merrily all the while, or take a long time because he is distracted by outside events?

Preschool children whose early temperament is negative and demanding are more likely to be diagnosed with ADHD as they get older. Temperament characteristics seen in the "difficult child," such as overactivity, high intensity, negative mood, and low adaptability, also are predictive of the continuation of ADHD into later childhood once they are developed. Temperament, while an important early risk factor for ADHD, can be improved or worsened by the type of environmental settings. The home environment combined with the child's temperament problems can increase the risk for later ADHD (Barkley, 1995).

Carey and McDevitt (1995), recognized researchers and writers on temperament, propose that when children are diagnosed with ADHD, for example, often the children simply present "normal temperament variations that do not fit at school and that nothing at all is wrong with their brains" (p. 147). They acknowledge that attention deficit does exist, but that the symptom of an attention deficit does not necessarily imply that the "standard syndrome is present" (p. 152). Their general premise is that most diagnoses are made from parent and teacher interviews and "never" from neurological examinations, and what is being called ADHD may in fact be at least in part a continuation of a difficult temperament interacting with the school setting. They suggest that a difficult temperament—while unpleasant—is not a disorder. Interventions will not change temperament, but temperament can be accommodated for by adaptive behaviors on the part of parents and schools. ADHD children are not representative of "the disorder itself but signs of a predisposition to develop difficulty in school" (Carey & McDevitt, 1995, p. 151).

Drawing from their famous New York Longitudinal Study based on clinical observations of children, Thomas, Chess, Birch, Hertiz, and Korn (1963) proposed nine characteristics of temperament. Out of these nine characteristics, Carey and McDevitt (1995) established three major clusters of the nine characteristics:

1. *The difficult child*, who is regular, slow to approach (withdrawing from novelty), slow to adapt, and intense, displaying much negative mood. This group represents about 10% of the study population.

2. *The easy child*, who is regular, approachable, adaptable, mild, and predominantly positive in mood. This group represents about 40% of the total group.

3. *The slow to warm up or shy child*, who is typically withdrawing in novel situations, slow to adapt, and low in activity and intensity, displaying much negative mood. These children represented about 5% to 15% of the study group.

As infants and young children, the difficult child is fussy, is difficult to soothe, and has problems with sleeping and eating. The child gets less positive attention from adults. The easy child, on the other hand, is very adaptable, playful, and responsive to adults. This child is likely to receive a great deal of positive adult attention since interactions with caretakers are positive and rewarding. The slow to warm up child is characterized by slow adaptability. This child is extremely shy in new situations and does not provide immediate responses to adults. Adults who sustain interactions with this child are usually rewarded with positive behaviors (Hooper & Umansky, 2004).

Carey and McDevitt (1995) suggest that what we label as ADHD is in fact temperament risk factors: being slow to adapt, being intense, and displaying negative mood, low persistence, high distractibility, and high intensity. "The practical significance of a child's temperament, therefore, resides in how it may or may not fit with the values and expectations of the caretakers" (Carey & McDevitt, 1995, p. 14). A child in a "poorness-of-fit" environmental setting would find himself or herself more challenged. Therefore, a teacher's preference can make different temperament characteristics more congenial or disruptive in the classroom setting. Ideally, what we would want for a child is a goodness-of-fit environmental setting to minimize the behaviors presented by the "difficult child." Carey and McDevitt argue that many individuals are being diagnosed with ADHD even though they do not have a disorder, but rather, a bad fit between temperament and environment in which a child is compelled to cope. ADHD, they suggest, should have a prevalence rate of less than 1% of the child population (Carey & McDevitt, 1995).

Caution With Diagnosis Based on Temperament

We will not attempt to debate "temperament" versus "ADHD disorder," but only recognize that whatever the label one wants to attribute to children manifesting ADHD symptoms, the behaviors do indeed present significant challenges to these children. Untreated ADHD can bring about negative long-term consequences. Remember, to be diagnosed with ADHD, a child must present significant problematic behaviors in more than one environmental setting. ADHD behaviors that occur only at school may be more of a sign of bad fit rather than a true disorder.

The medical model may not be the only model for understanding ADHD, but current research supports many of its findings and explanations. Recent research has put new light on how the brain functions and suggests that ADHD children present neurobiological delays in cognitive processes that contribute to learning, behavior, and emotional maturity. Medical providers and clinicians who work with ADHD children would not refute the role of temperament in a young child's adaptability. They recognize the importance of providing a good fit to help minimize ADHD traits; however, mental health practitioners also understand that environmental accommodations alone may not be enough to achieve maximum positive results. A difficult temperament, although an early risk factor for ADHD, is not the primary cause or primary contributor (Barkley, 1995).

Ideally, a diagnosis should help us better understand a child's behavior and should provide needed protections and rights not otherwise guaranteed. Our experience in working with families of ADHD children and teachers who teach these special children is that they would rather not debate terminology, but instead are looking for concrete suggestions to help achieve greater success with these children.

SUMMARY

By recognizing the symptoms and impairments of ADHD in preschool and early elementary children, teachers are more likely to be tolerant and understanding of the children's behaviors. Knowledge of the symptoms of ADHD and associated disorders, and how they exhibit themselves in the classroom, is the first step in responding properly to children who may need more attention, more acceptance, and more adapted instruction.

Developing and Reinforcing Appropriate Social Skills

3

Young children can show a wide range of healthy variability in the acquisition of skills such as language, self-control, attention and memory, and socialization. For children with ADHD or temperamental variations, preschool, kindergarten, and early school grades can be very challenging in the area of social skills development. This chapter reviews classroom settings that are especially problematic for children with ADHD and offers classroom interventions that can help improve their social skills.

When dealing with young children, it's important to remember that children younger than the age of eight should not be expected to apply problem-solving strategies to real-life situations very well without direct intervention. Children older than eight can benefit more from problem-solving instruction and will be more prone to apply these skills to real-life situations. Also, children who don't know how to comply or follow rules are not as receptive to problem-solving interventions. These children are better served by teaching compliance skills and utilizing discipline techniques: effective commands, warnings, positive and negative consequences, and time-outs (Bloomquist, 1996). Consequently, because of developmental limitations in young children, the interventions covered in this chapter focus on effective teacher-directed interventions and not so much on child problem-solving strategies.

It's important to remember that just because a child can come up with a plan, this doesn't necessarily mean the child can follow through with his or her plan. Teachers need to try to understand that young children are more challenged in mastering real-life situations than older children and their failures are not always representative of oppositional or motivational factors.

PRESCHOOL AND ELEMENTARY SCHOOL AS THE TRAINING GROUND

During early childhood, children increase the time that they spend in the company of others. Many preschoolers, for the first time, are developing peer friendships, working out power struggles, and learning to use language to settle disputes with adults and peers. Children also begin to form friendships and learn to take the perspective of others and acquire the ability to develop empathy. School becomes an important environment, outside the home, where children learn to work out problems, where they encounter rules and expectations of society, and where they can enhance self-awareness, social knowledge, and self-control. School becomes the place where children have the opportunity, outside of their home environment, to practice the skills necessary to develop these necessary social competencies. This is where they use the cognitive, behavioral, and communication skills necessary for the successful interpersonal interactions needed to develop friendships and positive self-esteem.

The Teacher's Role

For teachers, this critical period requires the implementation and understanding of effective classroom interventions for children with special needs, such as ADHD. Through appropriate classroom interventions, teachers can reinforce and teach appropriate social skills. The classroom environment provides an opportune setting, as the regularly occurring interactions of a typical classroom are effective in teaching the basic social skills necessary for social competency (Lavoie, 2005). In the learning environment, children can be taught directly the mechanics of learning how to join a group and how to establish and maintain friendships through classroom social interactions. Teachers can also directly influence a child's ability to learn how to resolve conflicts and to become aware of or "tune in" to social skills that occur around him or her.

Teachers can use positive behavior management strategies (such as contingent and consistent praise, ignoring and not criticizing, and the use of time-outs selectively when necessary to help a child regulate his or her behavior) in teaching and reinforcing appropriate social skills development in a young child.

Outside of the Classroom

Besides classroom lessons and activities, important social skills are learned at recess, in physical education, during school assemblies, on field trips, and in afterschool clubs such as Boy Scouts and sports teams. We cannot simply expect students to develop social skills because they have been put into social situations. They need direct instruction and understanding if we expect the child to find social competence or social acceptance. However, it's important to underline that in the absence of a positive and mutually rewarding relationship, children may not have adequate incentives to be cooperative, except possibly to receive a tangible reward (Campbell, 2002). Any long-term behavioral intervention must be built on mutual respect, genuine caring and understanding of the child's social difficulties, and parent involvement.

WHAT ARE SOCIAL SKILLS AND WHY ARE THEY SO IMPORTANT?

Childhood is the laboratory wherein the child uses trial and error to develop his or her repertoire of social skills (Lavoie, 2005). Social skills are those necessary skills that children must learn to have successful interpersonal interactions. They rely on a child's cognitive, behavioral, and communication skills. These skills can be broken down into *input, organization, output,* and *self-monitoring* (Rothenburg, 2005). Children with ADHD may struggle with aspects of each of these important skills. To successfully navigate the social skills maze, children must be able to understand the information that they are receiving, both the verbal and nonverbal nuances of an interaction. Then they must be able to organize this information into a category of sorts. They need to decide if the words they heard or the actions they saw mean that they should react or respond in a certain way. Then they must decide what the best response is to their perception about the information they now have organized. Last, they must evaluate if their response was appropriate or needs adjustment or changing (Rothenberg, 2005). This is quite a complicated process, and most children do learn how to implement these steps to maintain further social interactions.

A child with ADHD often does not have the skills or impulse control necessary to scan a situation and quickly determine the best way to become involved in a social interaction. They lack the ability to correctly perceive, interpret, and process the information from the world around them (Lavoie, 2005). That is why you may see this child run up to a "closed group" of individuals who may be talking to each other and hit someone in the group in an attempt to join the group. The child may not understand initially that the position of the group is a signal that they don't want anyone to join them at the time, nor does he or she realize or have the communication skills to inquire to see if the group is interested in having him or her join them. The consequence, because of developmental delays in disinhibiting behavior, can result in classmates not wanting to play with the child. The child will often be labeled by peers as a "troublemaker" or worse, by caretakers as a "behavior problem."

Long-Term Effects

The long-term effects of the lack of social skills are tremendous. A child's feelings about himself, his self-esteem, are often affected by his perceptions of how others react to him. If others react negatively and the child has difficulty interacting with peers, the child can suffer from feelings of rejection. This is often revealed in physical symptoms such as headaches, stomachaches, anxiety, and depression. The child may also express feelings of not wanting to go to school because he feels alienated and rejected by his classmates. Research has shown that the result of peer rejection often includes: significant early social difficulties and later risk for social and psychological maladjustment, including substance abuse and depressive disorders (Rothenberg, 2005).

The stakes are high for ignoring the social incompetence that children with ADHD exhibit. A primary need of human beings is to be liked and accepted by others. Children with social skills deficits do not act the way they do so that others will dislike them. According to Lavoie (2005):

> We must accept the unintentional nature of their behaviors and stop "blaming the victim." Once we realize this, we can see that punishing a child for social skill errors is ineffective, unfair and inappropriate. Punishing a child for social skills deficits is akin to punishing a child for nearsightedness or having the flu. The situation is beyond the child's control, so punishment simply won't work. (p. xxvi)

In light of this information, as educators, we must seize every opportunity to model and directly teach young children the skills and tools that they need to have successful social interactions. As teachers of young children, you will find this work sometimes difficult, but in the end very rewarding as you see these children begin to handle their own social situations once they have been taught the correct strategies to overcome their difficulties. We hope that the strategies shared in this chapter will help you and provide you with the tools you need to be successful in this endeavor.

Delayed Skills in Children With ADHD

For many preschoolers and early school-age children with ADHD, appropriate social skills are often delayed. Preschoolers at risk for ADHD behave more aggressively toward peers (Campbell, 2002), and young children who are impulsive and overactive are at risk for oppositional problems (Lavigne et al., 1996). It is often these behaviors that identify them with ADHD (Hooper & Umansky, 2004). These children struggle with the processing of and organization of verbal and nonverbal information. They have difficulty "reading" social situations and may take much longer to process a conversation. They may also direct their attention to irrelevant social cues or latch on to one facet of what someone has said, not getting the "gist" of the entire social interaction. They may also get lost in their own thoughts during a social interaction and lose interest in what the other person is saying. Sometimes, short-term memory problems cause these children to blurt out, as they are fearful that they will forget what they wanted to say (Rothenberg, 2005). Due to these difficulties, some of these children are not learning or being successful with the social skills they will need later when friendships depend on sharing, perspective taking, and common interests.

As discussed in Chapter 2, children with ADHD often disrupt the play of others and frequently shift from one activity to another. They tend to overreact and be impulsive in their interactions, which flood them with feelings that often result in aggression (Rothenberg, 2005). This pattern of negative interactions can lead to peer rejection.

SOCIAL SKILLS DEVELOPMENT

Problem-Solving Skills in Young Children

An important contributor to social skills development is learning problem-solving skills. In attempting to address this important developmental skill, programs such as *Second Step: A Violence Prevention Curriculum* address the area of problem-solving skills. *Second Step* is a research-based, classroom-based social skills program for preschool through junior high students. The focus of the program is to reduce impulsive, high-risk, and aggressive behaviors. Being able to solve problems and thinking about what you are doing is essential in life. One important step in problem solving is being able to stop and think before acting. Another important step is to think about what you are doing in a step-by-step manner while trying to solve a problem. Getting along with people involves developing good problem-solving skills. "Many children with behavior problems," writes Michael Bloomquist (1996):

are impulsive and are poor problem solvers. They may not recognize when a problem exists, they don't think ahead about the consequences of their behavior, they don't think of alternative ways to solve a problem, or, even if they think of a plan, they may not always follow the plan. (pp. 133–134)

Bloomquist goes on to write that children with social problems do not solve problems effectively. They are prone to make "mistakes" in perception, misinterpret others' behavior or intent, and blame others, accusing the other person of doing something "on purpose." They can have difficulty thinking of the problem from the other's point of view or putting the problem into perspective (Bloomquist, 1996, p. 134). Attention deficits affect a child's ability to observe, understand, and respond to his or her social environment (Lavoie, 2005). Young children with ADHD are challenged by many if not all of these factors.

STRATEGIES THAT SUPPORT SOCIAL SKILLS DEVELOPMENT

Problem-Solving Skills

By three to five years of age, peer groups become another source for teaching the child problem-solving skills as well as self-control. How preschool and early school-age children use constructive emotional coping and attentional control (distractibility) were positively related to boys' social skills and peer status in particular, whereas with girls, their use of avoidant coping methods was positively related to their social skills (Barkley, 1997). Consequently, it's doubly important to introduce social skills training to young children with ADHD because of their difficulties with age-appropriate attention control (distractibility) and emotional regulation.

Emotional Competence

All young children develop emotional competence that helps them in responding appropriately in social situations. According to Hooper and Umansky (2004), emotional competence has three components. These three components consist of emotional expression, emotional understanding, and emotional regulation. The successful mastery of these three cognitive processes helps lead to "emotional competence."

Emotional Expression

Emotional expression refers not only to how a child expresses emotions, but also an awareness of emotions. As children develop, the way they express their emotions changes from primarily crying to show discomfort to more flexible, complex, and differentiated modes (Hooper & Umansky, 2004). They might display a single emotion in a number of different ways; for example, happiness might be shown in a shy smile, or in exuberant jumping, laughing, and shouting. As children develop emotionally, they have more choices of emotions to choose from and more ways to show those emotions. Children with delayed emotional skills, like those with ADHD, might not have a very large repertoire of emotions to choose from and will show their discomfort and anger in highly emotional outbursts or "meltdowns."

Emotional Understanding

Emotional understanding refers to a young child's development of cognitive and language skills making him or her better equipped to understand his or her own emotions and those of others. Emotions serve as the vehicles that allow one person to have a sense of the mental state of another (Siegel, 1999). As children develop emotional understanding, they have words to label emotions rather than simply physically reacting to feelings that they cannot understand. Emotional understanding is complex, and even typically developing preschool-age children struggle with identifying their emotions with words or having the ability to recognize and understand the feelings of others. A young child who may have rudely grabbed a toy from another child really cannot relate when asked, "How do you think he feels when you take his toy away?" The child is barely able to label his own emotions and would have a very difficult time trying to figure out what another child feels.

Emotional Regulation

For children to be able to function in social situations, they must have the ability to regulate their emotions (Hooper & Umansky, 2004). *Emotional regulation* refers to a child's ability to adjust or change his or her emotions based on the situation, for example, adjusting from playground emotions to story-time emotions. The child needs to be able to adjust his or her emotions from the excitement of outdoor play to the inner calm for sitting quietly and attending. A child might also exhibit emotional regulation when he or she chooses not to hit the person who grabbed his or her toy, but rather glares at her instead. Typical children go through three steps when confronted with an emotion that needs regulating: first, they take notice of their emotions; second, they consider what the emotion means to them; and finally, they choose a response (Denham, 1998). Children with ADHD, who are impulsive, will have difficulty with going through all these steps before choosing a response. They often still cannot truly label their emotion, much less consider what it means before responding aggressively or, as some may see it, "inappropriately." Again, the key to remember is that social incompetence is a symptom of a disability and that punishment is not effective in teaching a child how to develop these skills.

FIVE PROBLEM-SOLVING AREAS THAT CHALLENGE CHILDREN WITH ADHD

Children with ADHD often need additional support and guidance to help them be more successful at ignoring, taking turns, sharing, and staying on task. Because of developmental delays in inhibition, a child with ADHD will often demonstrate developmental delays in these important skills.

Ignoring

Ignoring someone who is "bugging" you or teasing you can be difficult at times for both children and adults; however, ADHD children can be especially challenged with this important skill. ADHD children often ruminate or fixate on a thought or feeling and have difficulty regulating and recognizing their emotions. Consequently, they need more coaching and guidance in finding ways to ignore teasing or other negative behaviors. Young children often do best when they are coached on where to go, who to talk to, and what words to say when upset with a classmate's behavior.

Teachers need to be specific in terms of both expectations and suggestions to help the child. As an example, the teacher gives Bobby specific words and strategies to use when faced with a situation that would usually lead to negative behavior.

Teacher: Bobby, when Joey teases you, what did we talk about that you could do?

Bobby: I could say, "Stop, I don't like being teased!" Then I should walk away if Joey doesn't stop and talk to a teacher.

Teacher: Good. You are not to hit or yell, but walk away and find a teacher. Let's practice. I will pretend to be Joey and when I tease you, you will say "Stop, I don't like being teased," and then turn your back and walk away and pretend to find Ms. Smith, the yard duty teacher.

By teaching the child some simple words to say and then to walk away, you accomplish two important goals: first, you separate the children and improve the chance that the situation won't escalate, and second, you show that there are other choices besides hitting or yelling when teased.

The previous example uses a teasing situation as a problem-solving tool—to teach a form of ignoring. The child ignores his classmate by turning away if the teasing doesn't stop and then turns his attention to a behavior that can prevent a physical or verbal altercation.

It's again important to recognize that with young children, you will need to practice social skill activities, such as the one shown here, or use a social story to reinforce the concept, and always reinforce positive results more often than with older children.

Locus of Control

Also, unlike with older children, very young children need more external regulation and reinforcement. They often perceive consequences as the result of others, and not as something they have any control over. An important belief that children gain through experience is whether they themselves can control outcomes, that is, what developmentalists call "internal locus of control": the internal awareness that they can influence what happens to them. In very young children, they generally have not developed an awareness that luck, fate, or other people are not always in control of what happens to them. Children are said to have an "external locus of control" when they believe that events outside their control are responsible for what happens to them. When children believe that they can control the outcomes of their actions, that is, when they locate their control internally, they are more motivated to learn from their mistakes and are more reflective and self-directed learners (Porter, 2002). Consequently, very young children often have not developed the internal drive to practice for mastery and need outside direct instruction on how to control themselves. The use of role play and social stories can help students to learn this skill until they are intrinsically motivated to do so. Positive reinforcement and repetitive practice can support the development of these positive social skills.

Taking Turns

Taking turns is a give-and-take activity that requires high levels of self-control. Children with ADHD sometimes have difficulty with this activity because of developmental delays in inhibition. Turn taking is one of the basic commandments of childhood social success according to Lavoie (2005, p. 113). A child with ADHD will often find this task nearly impossible, often resulting in playing out of turn, pushing in line, or being impulsive while waiting for his or her turn at the computer. Affected children often can be disruptive, be provocative, and become aggressive waiting for their turn. This can especially be the case for boys, who are more likely to be aggressive. Because the child with ADHD often lacks the skills to engage in mutual turn taking, as well as listening, sharing, and responding appropriately in a social situation, he or she can be avoided or ignored by playmates in school, ending up isolated and rejected by peers.

When working with very young children, learning to take turns is often a social skill influenced by any number of factors from developmental differences to environmental influences, both at home and in school. Anyone who has worked with very young children recognizes that there is a wide range of differences in their ability to relate to the thoughts, desires, and feelings of others. Consequently, some children will be more receptive to interventions that help improve taking turns than others.

Like with "ignoring" activities, practicing or coaching a child in a real-life setting is helpful. As an example:

Teacher: Sally, you will need to put your hands to your side or in your pockets when standing in line to go to lunch.

Sally: Why, Ms. Smith?

Teacher: Because, Sally, when you line up for lunch, you get excited or impatient and start to push in front of a child ahead of you. Let's see when you wait with your hands to your side or in your pockets if you do better at waiting your turn in line.

This example is only one of many ways to help a child who is impulsive. Once the child knows what he or she is to do, it is an easier instruction to follow than the instruction, "Don't push, or don't touch." Keeping her hands to her side is a clear, concise action that is something that the child can do to improve her behaviors. The main point to remember is that children with ADHD are generally not "self-starters" or "self-stoppers." They need more reminders, explicit instruction, and monitoring than unaffected children do to stop a negative behavior or start a positive behavior. The child in the previous example, like many ADHD children, needs to practice interventions that minimize impulsivity and difficulties with delayed gratification.

Sharing

Affected children, like other young children, can share and play cooperatively with a classmate; however, children with ADHD can quickly become upset and no longer want to share a toy, book, or favorite puzzle. "Driven by the moment" and not taking time to think about their actions, they will grab a toy or book away from a classmate, telling them they no longer want to share. You may be saying, "Well, lots of young children don't like to share at times." That's true; however, affected children will present this pattern of behaviors more often than unaffected children of similar ages. You need to talk with the child ahead of time and go over the importance of his or her sharing when he or she is playing with a friend or working on a school project in the classroom. Again, reminders and coaching before the activity are important to minimize negative interactions. Often, it is wise to shorten the play or study period so the children can find more success. Because they get bored easily and have difficulty regulating their emotions, shortened time for interactive play or shared academic activities can help.

Staying on Task

It's both understandable and reasonable to expect very young children to have difficulty with focused and sustained attention. It's important to recognize that young children's attention span in general is short, and they can become easily distracted.

Many young children, unfortunately, are being asked to attend to tasks that they are not developmentally ready to tackle. We have found this especially true in settings in which very young children are introduced to academic material that is not developmentally appropriate. Consequently, what is seen as difficulty with staying on task is sometimes symptomatic of possible anxiety or avoidance behaviors stemming from introducing inappropriate academic materials, and not ADHD. Interesting, motivating, engaging, and appropriate instructional practices are the key to successful classroom management (Lavoie, 2005). Consequently, it is important to assess and make sure the activities are engaging and age appropriate.

SUGGESTIONS FOR REINFORCING APPROPRIATE SOCIAL BEHAVIORS

Although incentives to behave rarely work to improve a child's social incompetence, reinforcement can be extraordinarily effective. Reinforcement is the unexpected positive consequence of appropriate behaviors. Reinforcement and praise are fundamental to a child's mastery of social skills. Lavoie (2005) recognizes that parents and teachers must provide the Four R's of social development:

1. Reason: Provide a reason for the rule.

2. Rule: State the rule.

3. Reminder: Provide the child with a hint or memory trigger of some kind to remember the rule.

4. Reinforce: Recognize the appropriate behavior and give verbal praise. (p. xi)

One example might be as simple as, "The floors in the hallways are slippery, so you must walk when you are in the hallway. Remember, the floor is shiny like ice, so it is slippery like ice, which is why you need to walk when you are on the hallway floor. Thank you for choosing to walk in the hallway when you came in from recess. I appreciate you remembering how slippery it is." In this way, the rule is reinforced, and the child understands the rule and is verbally reinforced for following the rule. It is not always possible to reinforce verbally in a classroom with numerous young children, so the following quick verbal and nonverbal reinforcements are suggested.

Nonverbal Signs of Approval

- Giving a thumbs up
- Giving a pat on the head or shoulder
- Smiling
- Placing your arm around the child, indicating "good job"
- Nodding head in approval

Verbal Signs of Approval

- Great job!
- You did _____ very nicely!
- You did a terrific job remembering the rule!
- I like the way you ignored Joey.
- What a nice thing to do!
- You made a good choice.
- I will let your mom know you were able to sit on the square at Circle Time.
- Thank you for coming to the table the first time I called.
- I am happy to see you today.
- I am glad that you are here today.

As you can see from these verbal and nonverbal reinforcers, the message given to the child is that he or she is a valued individual. All children desire to be loved and accepted. The message that we need to send our students each and every day is that they are valued and accepted individuals. We need to try to catch them being good as an important way to reinforce positive social skills.

Social Stories

Carol Gray's *Social Stories™* program (http://www.thegraycenter.org) for children with autism has promise for all young children who struggle with social skills. Social Stories were created to help children with autism learn to "read" and understand social situations. These stories present appropriate social behaviors in the form of a story (Goldberg Edelson, 1995). These social stories provide the student an opportunity to participate in writing and reading a story about the child's own experience in a social situation. Carol Gray (Gray Center for Social Learning & Understanding, 2006) suggests that four types of sentences are utilized when writing a social story. The four types are: descriptive, directive, perspective, and control.

The following is a social story about going to recess.

After lunch we go to recess.—*Descriptive*

Sometimes recess is on the playground.—*Descriptive*

A lot of the children play on the playground equipment.—*Descriptive*

It is fun to play on the playground.—*Descriptive*

Everyone should play safely.—*Directive*

When the whistle blows, that means it is time to line up and go inside.—*Directive*

I will try to line up as soon as the whistle blows.—*Directive*

This will make my teachers happy.—*Perspective*

After I line up, I will try to stay in line—*Control*

Everyone will be proud of me!—*Perspective*

The social story describes a social setting, step-by-step directions for completing an activity that can be used to directly teach the appropriate behaviors for a social situation. The descriptive sentences describe what people do in a particular situation. The directive sentence in the social story directs the child to the appropriate response, stated in positive terms. The perspective sentence presents other children's reactions to a situation, so that the child can learn how other children might perceive various events or situations. The final sentence, or control sentence, might be added to help a child remember what they should do, and perhaps a strategy to help them remember the target skill of the social story.

Social stories can easily be created for young children who need help in developing control in high-emotion situations like learning to share, or in situations that may bring anxiety, like knowing what to do in a fire drill. Carol Gray (Gray Center for Social Learning & Understanding, 2006), the developer of social stories, suggests that for each directive or control sentence, there should be two to five descriptive or perspective sentences. With this in mind, social stories can be as simple as five sentences.

Figure 3.1   Example Page From a Social Story Using Mayer-Johnson Symbols

For students to learn the skills targeted in the social story, it is suggested that they "read" the story with an adult at least once a day after having the teacher read it with them at least twice to teach the content and to ensure comprehension. Young children with ADHD, who do not yet read, can benefit from the use of Mayer Johnson symbols, using the symbols and words to encode the content of each page of the story.

The student should continue to read the story at least once a day, probably before the time the social issues usually occur, for instance before recess or before free play time, to reinforce the appropriate social skills prior to going into that social situation. Once the teachers sees that the child has exhibited the appropriate social skill, the story can be faded from being read each day to a reminder only a few times a week. Many children who struggle with social skills and find themselves lost and frustrated with their lack of understanding of appropriate social responses will find these social story books a comfort and security blanket of sorts, as they can refer back to it when they are confused. As we have stated before, the misbehavior of these children is most often not willful, but rather stems from developmental delays in self-regulation, as well as arising out of frustration and confusion about how to act appropriately. Social stories provide a concrete example for how they should behave, making social interactions much less confusing and much more successful.

Using Children's Literature

Katherine DeGeorge (1998), a special educator, has found that utilizing children's literature to teach the concepts of appropriate social skills is an effective practice, especially in the area of helping children with mild disabilities to understand the rules of friendship and social interaction. She feels that "through the use of children's literature, children with mild disabilities can be taught valuable skills that will enable them to make and maintain friendships." She has found in her own experience that using children's literature is a resource for instruction that also incorporates other academic tasks. She finds that the skills are more meaningful to the students through the stories they read. The models of the characters in the stories provide models that they are able to use outside of the regular classroom activities.

Teaching Friendship Skills

Literature provides an opportunity to learn important literacy skills, but it can also be utilized to show how children relate to each other in situations that a young child can relate to. Using children's literature as a model, students are directly instructed to follow the five steps after watching the teacher model:

- Identify someone to whom you can introduce yourself
- Smile and approach the person
- Introduce yourself
- Ask open-ended questions to get and give information
- Suggest something to play or do together

This type of direct instruction is necessary with frequent modeling of examples of appropriate ways to follow these steps and "non-examples" of inappropriate ways of introducing oneself to another person. Students need to see what we mean and what we don't mean. They may think it is funny when the teacher models running up to and attempting to get to know someone by pushing, but students will remember that behavior is an inappropriate way to meet someone. Direct instruction on introduction addresses one of the key social skills identified by Richard Lavoie (2005). He states that "the strategies a child uses to join a group of peers participating in an activity will largely determine whether he will be accepted or rejected by others" (p. xxxii). If students can learn specific step-by-step strategies using children's literature and specific scripted practice, young children with ADHD should be able to develop this all-important social skill.

CHALLENGING SETTINGS FOR CHILDREN WITH ADHD

Teachers say they are regularly provided workshops on academic readiness and school-based curriculum, but find that there is much less, if any time, devoted to trainings on social skills and behavioral management of children in challenging school settings. The consequence, generally, is that each teacher is left to his or her own initiative and expenses in finding ways to help children better manage themselves in school settings.

The most frequent and challenging settings in school are related to transitions from one activity to another, unstructured times such as recess and lunch, as well as naptime for preschool children. Other problem settings are large-group instruction time, like "circle time" in a preschool classroom, or general instruction time in an early elementary classroom. Recognizing that these settings put a child with ADHD at risk for socially inappropriate behaviors should help you as an educator to be prepared for these difficult times. Being aware of the times that are difficult for this child will help you prepare the child ahead of time through the strategies previously discussed in this chapter. Once you are able to recognize the settings or activities that are problematic, proactive behavior management strategies can be employed. The teacher can prepare the child through role plays, scripts, problem solving, and social stories to prepare for social interactions that may be difficult for him or her. Recognizing these following areas will help both the teacher and the child to have more positive days together and will teach the child the all-important skills needed to succeed at school.

Transitioning

Transitioning from one setting to another can be challenging for children with ADHD, as these are times of less structure. When changing from circle time to stations, or when moving from the classroom to recess or outdoor play, children with ADHD struggle with knowing how to act appropriately in these less-structured times. They struggle with the difficulties that come from being overly focused on what they are currently doing, which makes changing to a new activity hard for them, and from being internally distracted and not paying attention to the instructions for the transition. Others have a hard time with transitions, as they are "driven by the moment" and find that movement time in the classroom is a time when excitable emotions can drive behavior that will often result in behavior that seems inappropriate.

Children with ADHD often will run or carelessly discard what they were doing to rush to the next activity they find more interesting or exciting. They will transition, but not in a manner the teacher may appreciate. Because of developmental delays in inhibiting behavior and self-directed talk (internalized speech), they don't stop or tell themselves to complete what they are doing before moving to another project or activity. Also, "driven by the moment," they don't stop to measure the consequences of their actions. Even though they have been reminded many times before to put the toy away before going to the next center, toss their finished lunch in the trash, or put their worksheet in their desk, they seem not to remember. They can make the same mistake over again, leading to teacher and parental frustration.

Consequently, children with ADHD require more reminders than unaffected children. It's important to emphasize that the child's forgetting to remember is often not purposeful, but is a common trait seen in children with ADHD. Here are some suggestions to help with children's "driven by the moment" behaviors:

- Reinforce the student (with a tangible reward or verbal praise) for changing from one activity to another without difficulty.
- Be clear with the student about class rules related to transitioning.
- Ask the parent to practice transitioning behaviors from low-interest to high-interest tasks (watching TV to setting the kitchen table). The parent can practice classroom transitioning tasks such as walking from the living room to the kitchen.
- Practice problem behaviors at home so the child can be more successful at home (walking, standing in line, not interrupting a sibling who is talking).
- Be clear about what you *want* the child to do during a transition rather than what you don't want them to do. It is easier for children to "keep their hands at their sides" than to "not touch other people," or to "walk" rather than "not run."

Difficulty Controlling Emotions

Children with ADHD often have little patience when asked to do something they don't like to do. They can quickly lose their temper, can fall down on the floor, can yell at the teacher, and commonly are observed saying "no" more than once. In a nutshell, their mood can go from a child who seems contented and cooperative to a child who becomes oppositional and hard to manage.

Children with ADHD, because of delays in inhibition, often say or do what first comes to their mind without stopping to think about the consequences. Consequently, it is helpful to give the child a warning, whenever possible: "You will need to put your truck away when the bell rings in a few minutes" or "We will be stopping work on our math sheet and opening up our reading book in five minutes." Children may need a reminder every minute to prepare them for the fact that they will need to change activities or transition soon, along with short reminders on what behaviors are expected. Affected children need more external reminders than unaffected children because of developmental delays in emotional and behavioral self-regulation.

Suggested Ways to Help Temper Negative Emotions

- Always provide transitional warnings, so that the child can prepare mentally and emotionally for the change from one activity to another.
- Reinforce the student for demonstrating anger management by providing tangible rewards (e.g., being line leader, passing out materials, having extra time on the computer).
- Write up a contract specifying what behaviors are expected (walking away when angry, asking for the teacher's help, going to a quiet spot).
- Reinforce the child for using a strategy that helped him or her control his or her emotions.
- Maintain close proximity to the student when transitioning.
- Be aware of what activities or situations are particularly problematic, and provide coaching in these areas to help the student be more successful.
- Maintain close communication with the parent on the student's progress (giving a token at home for positive anger management, speaking with the doctor if emotional outbursts seem especially elevated).
- Remind yourself that the child's difficulty with regulating emotions is often driven by chemistry as much as by environment.
- Understand that an emotional meltdown is not directed at you, but rather is a result of the child being unable to control his or her own anger, frustration, and emotions.
- Provide the child with "minor choices" when transitioning, so that he or she can feel somewhat in control. Allow the child the choice to sit on the floor or a chair when sitting in circle time.

Circle Time

Sitting quietly and paying attention during circle time can be another challenging time for a young child with ADHD. The lack of structure that comes from sitting on the floor with no defined space creates a situation in which you often will find preschool and kindergarten children pushing against each other, shouting out before being called on, or rolling around on the floor. The child with ADHD, because of hyperactive and inattentive behaviors, is challenged to "be good" during circle time. The affected child can attend for short periods at times, but generally becomes quickly bored and will start to fidget, talk out, or stand up.

Strategies to help the child attend in circle time include having the child sit close to the teacher so he or she can be monitored and frequently reinforced when cooperating. This arrangement allows the child to help turn pages in a book or help hold up a display to keep engaged. Another choice, sometimes successful, is to let the child sit inside a hula hoop instead of on an unmarked spot on the floor. The child is told he can move around inside the hula hoop, but cannot have any body part (hands, feet) outside the hula hoop. Another option is to have the child sit in the back of the circle on a chair instead of on the floor. The structure of the chair alone often helps the child attend and also allows some movement without distracting those around him. Another option for helping children with ADHD sit in a chair for longer periods of time is to allow them a cushion, like a Disco Sit, which allows them to move slightly, providing a release for motoric movement without disturbing others.

Sometimes letting the child fidget or play with an object in his or her hands, such as a Cushy Ball or other fidget toy, can help the child attend through circle time. This fidget toy can help the child redirect his or her elevated activity level and improve his or her ability to attend, making circle time a more successful time for all involved.

Naptime

Naptime can especially be a problem for preschool children with ADHD. Affected children have difficulty settling down, and getting them to fall asleep can become nearly an impossible task. They generally require close monitoring by staff, which takes up extra time and attention. You can find the child with his feet in the air, moving on and off his cot, sitting up, lying down, and pulling on his covers, but seldom closing his eyes and falling asleep. This child needs the accommodation of a quiet "rest time" to read a book, color, or play with a small toy. Even with this accommodation, the child may become bored quickly with rest time, so plan on the child needing other options. If the program permits, moving the child to a room where there is no naptime can help. When naptime is over, the child can return to his homeroom.

Sometimes a gentle back rub or sitting close by the child can help him or her settle down and hopefully fall asleep. A backrub can help elevate those neurotransmitters that can help calm his or her body and make it ready for rest.

Playtime

Play is an important developmental activity for young children, but due to the lack of structure for play, it can be difficult for young children with ADHD. Despite these difficulties, play persists as the main vehicle for child development until other activities take its place, and play holds an extremely important place in the development of a child's social skills. Play is not only enjoyable and entertaining to a young child, but it has numerous benefits as well. Play advances children's physical development, it allows children to build knowledge and skills that help in problem solving, and play precedes the advent of language—it is instrumental in helping children learn language. Play puts children in an environment where they must employ communication skills and begin to master speech. It helps them to build good self-esteem (they can control events in their world), helps build confidence, and promotes persistence, self-restraint, and creativity. Last, play is instrumental in helping children to socialize. Through play, children learn their culture's role expectations and rules as well as what behaviors are acceptable (Porter, 2002). Through play, children learn to control aggressive tendencies and to develop prosocial behaviors (e.g., altruism, empathy, and cooperation). Play is the "laboratory" where children learn new skills and practice old ones (Teeter, 1998).

Children with ADHD need all of these benefits of play, but also may need the close monitoring and modeling of teachers in the play setting to learn the appropriate prosocial skills necessary to be successful for play. Playtime for these young children will require the assistance of adults in the play setting to model problem-solving strategies and appropriate use of language skills to obtain what they want. Playtime can be a tremendous social skills training ground if the teacher is involved in guiding and directing this extremely beneficial learning environment.

Recess and Lunchtime

Just as with playtime, young children with ADHD need the intervention of teachers and other adults to help them navigate through the uncertainties and emotions of a typical recess or lunchtime. When a highly impulsive, emotionally charged child heads out to recess without a plan or without rehearsing options for unstructured time outside, difficulties with appropriate social behaviors are bound to happen. These children, who do not have the ability or executive functions of prioritizing, sequencing, and self-monitoring to revert to a self-corrected "Plan B" if their original plan is disturbed, will be found grabbing the ball from another child if they went out with a mindset to play with the ball. They will not be able to self-regulate and figure out what other options might be. The role of the teacher is to help them come up with a plan for recess or lunch. They will need direct instruction on what to do if someone else already has the ball or is already on the tricycle. They will need to practice the things they will say and the actions that they will take. They might need to carry a social story with them that will remind them what to do, and they will *always* need an adult who they can go to who will help them figure out the next steps when they are unable to figure it out themselves. They will need to be frequently reinforced when they make good choices like coming to a teacher for help. These teacher "interruptions" at recess should be viewed just like any other instructional period. Teachers would not become upset with a child for asking the name or sound of a letter during an instructional time, so in the same vein, teachers must be patient with children at recess who need them to help them mediate the social interactions that they must master on the playground.

SUMMARY

Being aware that certain settings require greater social skills should help teachers recognize when proactive strategies are required for the child with ADHD. School can be more enjoyable when teachers realize that with a few accommodations and adaptations, these children can be as successful as their peers.

Children with ADHD can be successful, but they need more support from their teachers in monitoring and coaching to develop social competence. These children desire, like everyone else, to belong, and with your understanding, you can help prevent feelings of low self-esteem and a sense of victimization. Through carefully planned instruction that is sequenced and reinforced, you can be one of the most important change agents in a child's life. As an educator, you have inherited one of life's most important jobs—the teaching of a child's educational and social skill development.

Help, This Kid Is Driving Me Crazy!

4

Proactive Classroom Management and Positive Behavior Supports

Daniel enters the classroom door for the first day of the next 16 years of his educational career. He looks clean, almost shiny, and excited to be here on his first day of preschool. He is wearing his new Spider Man shirt, new shorts, and brand new, light-up tennis shoes. The backpack, which is empty except for his snack of carrots and juice, also sports a bright red Spider-Man. Next to trucks, Spider-Man is his favorite!

Daniel scans all the fun items filling the classroom. There are trucks, yes, trucks! There are blocks, a kitchen and dress-up area, a table with playdough, a table with coloring items, and a place with beanbag chairs and books. Daniel decides that yes, although school has sounded a bit scary, it might just be fun after all. He gives his worried mother a quick kiss goodbye, drops his backpack carelessly on the floor, and heads over to the trucks. He finds some of his favorites. The dirt carrier and the bulldozer are not being used by anyone; he grabs them and starts driving them around the carpet making his truck noises. This is really fun, he thinks to himself, and he does not hear the teacher ring a small triangle and call all the children to the carpet by the beanbag chairs because he is busy imagining his trucks taking down mounds of dirt and loading mountains of dirt to take to some distant jobsite. He imagines being the truck driver and hearing the roaring engines, he thinks about the smell of dirt . . . when suddenly he realizes that the teacher is now standing next to him looking displeased at him. He is not sure why, and the anxious thought that maybe this isn't going to be fun creeps into the back of his mind.

The teacher takes his hand and leads him to the carpet where all the other children are already sitting. They are all staring at him, and he feels uncomfortable. The teacher seats him near her feet and begins talking about rules, the calendar, what day of the week it is, and what they will be learning. They talk again about the rules and the triangle noise and sitting "criss-cross, applesauce." He tries to do it, but finds that it is hard to keep his feet tucked in just right, and he soon has his legs splayed out in front of him. He tries to listen about the days of the week, but is not sure just what they are and what the lady is talking about. His mind starts wandering back to the trucks and without thinking, he is again on the carpet playing with the trucks and making truck noises. This time when he sees that lady's feet and looks up, he sees more than displeasure, he sees anger and frustration. She reminds him of the rules about "criss-cross, applesauce" and how he cannot get up without permission. She tells him that if he gets up again without permission, he will be sent to time-out. He is not sure what this is, but he does know that it does not sound good.

And so Daniel has begun his educational career. Within the first hour of his first day in the first year, he has become anxious and uncomfortable, and he has been identified as a defiant child. Will things get better for him? Will his preschool experience help him get his impulses under control? Will time-out and "criss-cross, applesauce" prepare him for the career ahead of him? Only with the knowledge, expertise, and understanding of his teachers, parents, and friends who understand that Daniel has a real disability (ADHD) and that this disability makes him different, but not bad, will he find the road ahead of him a positive, successful one rather than a demeaning one that leads to negative self-esteem and a lifetime of failure.

Daniel is not unlike many other four-year-olds who enter preschool. His parents would describe him on the teacher information forms as energetic, curious, fun loving, and caring. He likes to play outside with trucks, likes to climb everything, and loves to ride his tricycle. His history has not been without problems though, but his parents are not going to write this on the information sheet. He has not been invited to the neighbors' birthday parties because often, during early play dates, Daniel would be impulsive and grab toys from others and would be unwilling to share. He bit more than one friend and hit quite a few of them. He had his share of temper tantrums and meltdowns when he did not get his way. His parents secretly hope that the preschool experience will help him with his social skills shortcomings. They hope that with structure and more opportunities to play with other children, Daniel will learn to control himself and develop more friendships.

This chapter has been written for all of the Daniels who will enter your classroom during your teaching career. You might now even be thinking of one. Most people can; usually the whole school knows who they are almost instantly. Hopefully, the strategies that you learn in this chapter and throughout this book will help you as you learn to develop a philosophy of behavior management that is a positive one.

DEVELOPING A PERSONAL PHILOSOPHY OF BEHAVIOR MANAGEMENT

Why is it important to have a personal philosophy of behavior management? When the kids are driving you crazy and Daniel has not followed directions for the umpteenth time today, you need a philosophy—almost like a religious faith that you can hold close and that will get you through those times when you want to throw in the towel or strangle that kid! Charles, Lavoie, and other experts on classroom management and students with special needs share the premise that all teachers need to develop such a philosophy of behavior management (Charles, 2005; Lavoie, 1996a). The most important fact to remember is that all students are different and that every child is unique. Although all four-year-olds may be similar in some respects, they do individually differ from other four-year-olds. Because of this truth, no single set of rules for behavior management is effective under *all* conditions with *all* children (Walker, Shea, & Bauer, 2004).

Understanding Behavior Management

Perhaps you have never really thought about a specific behavior management philosophy or what your beliefs are about behavior management. Before you decide or reflect on what your philosophy might be, here are a few ideas on what behavior management really is (see Form 4.1). According to Walker et al. (2004), "Behavior management is the action(s) that teachers and parents engage in to enhance the probability that others will develop effective behaviors that are personally fulfilling, productive and socially acceptable" (p. 7). The goal of behavior management is not so much compliance as it is teaching a child appropriate behavior and actions to be accepted as a member of society. These skills are developed with what is best for the child in mind and must be looked at as a work in progress. Young learners will be developing appropriate behavior skills throughout their lifetime. It won't happen during the first month of school.

Reflecting on Your Philosophy

We'll now go through the statements one by one to get a sense of what each one means for you and your students.

It is only fair that all students follow the same set of rules.

If you find that you agree with this, then your classroom probably has the consistency and structure that children with ADHD may need. You may also find that your students with ADHD need some clearly understood and agreed-on modifications to those rules based on their development and specific needs.

Following rules should really depend on the situation.

If you find that you agree with this, you have probably already allowed for the specific individual needs of students with ADHD or other disabilities in

Form 4.1   Behavior Management and Classroom Discipline Beliefs

What are your beliefs about behavior management and classroom discipline?

- ☐ It is only fair that all students follow the same set of rules.
- ☐ Following rules should really depend on the situation.
- ☐ Following consistent rules is important, but at times, rules may need to be adjusted.

Write your own thoughts about how you identify your philosophy of behavior management:

What did you learn about your own philosophy of behavior management?

your classroom. You may also find that your students with ADHD need clear, concise, and well-understood rules and agreed-on consequences for when they do not follow the rules as prescribed.

Following consistent rules is important, but at times, rules may need to be adjusted.

If you find that you agree with this, you've likely already developed a positive, safe learning environment for all of your students. You will probably find that you do have clearly defined behavioral expectations and that you have made modifications for students with ADHD and other special needs.

If you find that you are not sure of what your behavior management philosophy is, there are some key principles (Charles, 2005) to help guide you in determining one (use Form 4.1 to work through this process):

- Reflect on and clarify how you want your students to behave now and in the future.
- Establish conditions in the classroom that encourage those behaviors.
- Plan how to help students become the kind of people you hope they will be, and decide on the actions you can take to help them conduct themselves acceptably.

Charles (2005) also encourages you to think about and plan ways that you can intervene in a helpful manner when misbehavior occurs.

Deciding on Rules for Behavior

When teachers make decisions about rules and expectations for classroom behavior, they need to keep the concept of teaching new behavioral skills in the forefront of their thinking (Walker et al., 2004). They need to determine if that particular rule or behavioral policy allows the student to learn a new, more appropriate skill that will help them become better citizens, or is the rule or policy simply intended to stop a behavior? If the most common response to behavior is time-out or removal from the classroom, the student is not learning a new behavior that will make him or her more successful in the future. Helping the students solve problems through choice making gives them the opportunity to develop a problem-solving skill that they can always carry with them.

The Rights of Children

The rights of children should serve as the foundation of all behavior management decisions made by all teachers. Teachers must follow the principles of fairness, and for children like Daniel, that means providing him with what he needs rather than what is the same or equal treatment of the other students (Walker et al., 2004). All decisions about Daniel's specific behavior management strategies should be made from the point of view of what is best for him and his social development. This might mean that Daniel needs extra redirection or needs a special seat or fidget to carry with him to keep his hands busy. These accommodations are fair for Daniel because they may be what Daniel needs to be able to attend to learn in your classroom.

Fair Versus Equal

It is important to point out that *fair* and *equal* are very different. Most of us equate the words as having similar meanings, but equal and fair are not the same (Lavoie, 1996a). It is hard for students and teachers to recognize these differences and not feel like they are "cheating" when they are giving Daniel an extra direction or opportunity that others do not have. Many worry that the students will think it is "not fair" if Daniel gets to sit on the special cushion or stand while he works. Incredibly though, children (especially young children) are very accepting of their classmates' differences. Simply explaining that Daniel needs the cushion or needs to stand is often enough of an explanation. They may want to try it out and see what it is like and then will move on and not worry about why Daniel has something different than they do. It is usually the teachers who struggle more with perceived inequity than students do.

Children like Daniel need to be accepted for who they are: a young person with a disability. Just as a teacher would not refuse the use of a ramp to a young child in a wheelchair, teachers must also provide the accommodations or extra patience necessary to help the child with ADHD be a successful student. The important point here is that we must respect the dignity of these children, be tolerant of who they are, and provide them with classroom opportunities that allow them to be as successful as their peers. These children will not change through criticism, punishment, or other punitive measures (Charles, 2005). To pull this off, teachers need to be familiar with ADHD, understand how it affects each individual child, and know what each particular child needs to have a positive, normal school experience.

Demonstrating Respect

Ultimately, all children deserve the teacher's respect. Respect is shown and communicated to the child when the teacher understands his or her strengths, desires, and weaknesses. The child will know respect and will feel safe in the classroom if the child realizes that he or she will be treated with consistency and respect (Canter, 1996). In a classroom where respect reigns, students need not fear physical punishment, sarcasm, isolation, punitive remarks, or inconsistencies in daily routine and behavioral expectations. In a climate of acceptance, dignity, respect, and encouragement, discipline problems become increasingly insignificant (Charles, 2005). In the classroom where the child knows that he or she is safe, there are specific principles of classroom order.

The Positive Classroom Environment

The positive classroom has an environment that is based on positive behavior reinforcement. Simply put, that is recognizing when the child has done something correct and providing positive reinforcement for this appropriate action or behavior (Walker et al., 2004). This is built on the premise that positive reinforcement changes behavior, whereas negative reinforcement only stops behavior (Lavoie, 1996a). Positively reinforcing the behavior that you want, through words or tokens, increases the likelihood that the behavior that you want to occur will happen again (Walker et al., 2004). In this sense, students feel that you approve of them and their attempts to follow your directions and behave in the manner that you request. On the following pages are suggestions for what makes a learning environment a positive one.

Predictable and Consistent

A positive learning environment can be achieved by planning on creating classroom order that is predictable and consistent from day to day. A calm, structured, positive learning environment that is uncluttered and well organized allows students with ADHD to be less distracted and anxious (Charles, 2005). Up to 25% of students with ADHD struggle with anxiety as a coexisting condition (American Academy of Pediatrics, 2006). This anxiety is increased when they do not know what will be happening next. You will often find that these children will ask you what they will be doing next and what time they will have lunch or recess. They are not trying to be pesky, nor do they really just live for lunch and recess. These times hold activities that are familiar to them, and they find comfort in knowing when those things are coming. When they don't know what will happen next, they are more likely to become agitated and begin to wander and look very much off task, as they are not regulated enough to think about a quiet activity to engage in until the teacher gives the next order. To solve this problem, a consistent daily routine through the use of the daily agenda is key to quelling these fears (Charles, 2005). For students who do not read, a visual agenda can be provided using Mayer-Johnson visual symbols to help them recognize what activity will happen next

---

Example of a Daily Agenda

Preschool Classroom	**Elementary Classroom**
Centers	Warm-up journal write
Circle time	Math meeting—calendar
Table work	Math
Recess	Math stations
Snack time	Recess
Music	Spelling
Story time	Reading
Closing centers	Lunch
	Library
	Science—animal research
	Clean-up/homework

(Mayer-Johnson, n.d.; see Figure 4.1). When the children see what their day entails, they are more likely to easily transition from one activity to another and be mentally ready to start the next activity that is planned.

Keeping the Structure and Routine

Along with the agenda, specific daily routines are key to the success of students with ADHD. When students understand that from day to day, the order of activities, the specific routine for each activity, and the behavioral expectations for each activity remain the same, students again are less anxious. Through repetition, they will learn to follow directions and comply with the behavioral expectations through daily practice. Routines can include such strategies as lining up before entering the classroom, giving instructions prior to entering the room, or doing a warm-up activity prepared for students before they enter the room each day (Rief, 1998). For preschoolers, this might be specific centers set up with directions on which center to go to first; for older students, this could entail either an activity at their desks or one provided on the board or overhead. This clear expectation that students enter the room and go right to work keeps problems from occurring when students enter and may not be sure what to do next. Students with ADHD will find something of interest to occupy themselves, and this may not be what the teacher wants them to do.

Clear and Concise Instructions

Other strategies include giving specific directions, naming exactly what you want the child to do. An example might include: "Sit at the yellow table with your hands flat on the table." The next direction would not be given until all students have complied with the first one, providing "wait time" for students to comply. Once the first action has been completed, the students would be given the next direction, such as, "Pick up one colored marker and write the letters in your name." This *chunking* of directions into small parts helps students who have difficulties with following multiple-step directions due to distractibility and short-term memory deficits (Levine, 2002). Levine (2002) reports that short-term memory allows for very brief retention, usually two seconds for new information. Short-term memory allows information to move into working memory in chunks, where most children recode it into chunks. Children with attentional issues may not be paying attention to the most important chunks of information and find that they are lost. Chunking also helps the teacher see who is having difficulties actually executing the tasks requested. If students struggle with the tasks even after these simple directions, the teacher now knows that it is not the inability to follow directions, but rather a problem with the difficulty of the task.

Figure 4.1   Visual Agenda Using Mayer-Johnson Symbols

Form 4.2   Daily Agenda

What would the daily agenda look like in your classroom?

Write out the activities of your day in the space provided below:

Remember that the exact time of each activity is not as
important as the order and consistency in which the activities occur!

ANALYZING BEHAVIOR

Witnessing a child like Daniel blatantly push another child out of his or her seat during an assigned writing time brings most teachers to shake their head and consider sending him to the office one more time. They cannot seem to figure out why he sometimes acts that way, and the behavior is often enough to make them want to have him exiled to the office forever! Of course, Daniel will not be able to tell the teacher why he did it, and may even deny doing *anything*. Why is he so frustrating? Yes, it is frustrating, and at times, it seems to make no sense why he acts the way he does. In reality, there is usually some cause for the behavior that we do not immediately recognize.

What Is the Behavior Communicating?

As teachers, it is our job to take a step back and look at the behavior from a nonemotional observer's perspective. What happened right before the behavioral outburst? Does this outburst occur around the same time each day? Does it always happen around a particular child? Does it happen in a particular part of the room? Analyzing the situation will often reveal the real reason for his somewhat bizarre and unpredictable behavior (Lavoie, 1996a). If you are unable to observe, you might ask a college student or an assistant to just observe his behaviors for a few days to identify any patterns. Other patterns or observations that Lavoie (1996a) suggests in a "situational analysis" is observing what classroom activities were occurring, what time of day the behavior occurred, or if there were significant factors such as fatigue, hunger, temperature, noise, medication, or illness.

For some children with ADHD, it is not uncommon to find that the behavior is intended to cover up some academic deficit. "Many students would rather be viewed as bad than dumb any day" (Lavoie, 1996a, p. 7). For this reason, it is important to observe if misbehavior or significant off-task behavior is occurring only during specific instructional time, or during the part of the day when a specific content area is covered. The student may be trying to cover up his or her inability to follow directions or complete a task by acting out. They may find that being removed from the classroom or being reprimanded takes the pressure off, and they get out of doing the academic task that they cannot figure out how to do.

Why Doesn't He or She Ask for Help?

This leads to another common problem that children with ADHD and learning disabilities face. You would think that if they don't know what to do, they would simply ask. Unfortunately, these students often have difficulties with forming questions. This weakness in "interrogation" leaves students without the skill to get the help that they need (Lavoie, 1996b). These students will push the assigned paper back at you or onto the floor, muttering, "This is stupid," simply because they may not be able to understand the written directions and do not know how to ask you to explain it to them. We see the behavior as defiance and a lack of motivation, but it is simply an inability to figure out how to form questions. If you take that step back again and become the observer, you will probably realize that this is a student who rarely if ever raises his hand with a question. He doesn't do it because he doesn't know how.

How do you remedy this? Many students with ADHD, as you may have already noticed, may have a very difficult time getting started on tasks. After a few trips to the pencil sharpener, drinking fountain, tissue box, and restroom, work on the task might begin, but probably very likely behavior will begin. This is not due to laziness, but rather due to confusion about what the task entails and the inability to ask how to do it. An effective strategy would include standing near the child and repeating the directions written at the top of the page, or explaining the directions given to the whole class individually. Staying near their desk while they work through the first task and then reinforcing them if they are correct, or redirecting them if they are wrong, will ensure that they understand what the task entails without making them ask for help. Once you are sure that they are on the right track, you can move away and simply make a few sweeps by later to see that they are still on the right track. Why is it important to provide this support in getting started? Anxiety about the inability to do what you ask is one of the causes of the behaviors that you find so often disrupt your class. Reducing anxiety by ensuring that they understand what is expected in a given task should provide you with calmer and more on-task behavior.

The Squeaky Wheel *Needs* the Grease

"It is the squeaky wheel that needs the grease," according to Rick Lavoie (1996a, p. 9). If you look at the fact that the behavior that may be driving you crazy is actually an attempt to communicate an unmet need to you, you may find that you have fewer days where you leave work frustrated. If you look at finding out what the behavioral need is, like a detective, you will find that you are not so emotionally involved and hurt by the behavior, but rather on the path to finding out what type of grease is needed to fix the squeak. The student who acts out actually sees you as a person who cares enough to help him or her. Unfortunately, these students cannot always use words to identify their needs and, instead, let their behavioral outbursts speak for them. So if you'll indulge us here, we could say that he is driving you crazy because he really likes you and knows that you care about him.

PUTTING THE STRATEGIES TO PRACTICE

If we go back to Daniel and his apparent defiance on the rug, experts would surmise that his behavior was probably not due to deliberate defiance (Charles & Senter, 2005). In observing his behavior, one may realize that he is not able to sit comfortably in a "criss-cross, applesauce" position and really needs to spread his legs out. One could also figure out that some of the concepts being discussed are not concrete enough for a four-year-old developing mind to grasp. He may not have an understanding of the calendar, time, and the days of the week. So now that we understand the "why" of his behavior, what do we do about it?

First, we go back to the fact that fair and equal are not the same thing. Fair is getting what you need; it does not mean getting the exact same thing as others. To be fair to Daniel, he might need to sit in a chair in the back of the group. He might need to sit on a carpet square so that he understands his own space; he may need to be allowed to sit inside a hula hoop allowing him the room he needs to stretch out his legs and not touch others. He might need a teacher near him to use a gentle touch to keep him grounded in his seat. Although he might not yet understand time concepts, he can be involved in putting numbers on the calendar and counting orally. He might need to sing songs about the days of the week and the months of the year to become familiar with them. In doing these activities, he is developing the prerequisite skills to be able to understand the concepts of time when he is cognitively ready. To keep him engaged in circle time, you might have him be the person who checks the weather or takes the attendance to the office. He might hold a fidget toy in his hands while he listens to others and waits his turn. He might be allowed to stand and move his body or do hand symbols or movement exercises while counting and singing. Providing instructional strategies that are motivational and engaging will help him remain included. As you can see, there are many ways to keep Daniel active, engaged, and positive about his daily circle time experience.

Proactive Discipline

To manage behaviors proactively rather than reactively, one must anticipate that problems and difficulties will occur for children with ADHD in the classroom. Canter and Canter (1993) define *proactive discipline* as anticipating misbehavior and planning in advance how to deal with it in a positive manner. On the other hand, "Reactive discipline is defined as waiting until the student misbehaves and *then* determining what to do to get them back on course" (as cited in Charles, 2005, p. 39, emphasis added). Recognizing that certain activities or changes in routines or academic requirements are going to be challenging to the child will help you be prepared and understand the behavior and be proactive when it occurs. Anticipating problems and difficulties will help you not get emotionally involved and will make the behavior less frustrating to you as the teacher. Unfortunately, reactive discipline occurs when we are not ready for a behavior and are too emotionally involved to be able to step back and look at the behavior and what it is communicating objectively. This will happen to all of you! At times like this, it is best to call a colleague to take over for a few minutes so that you can take care of your own emotions before trying to deal with a student's meltdown or behavioral outburst. Staying calm, not speaking for a moment or two, and breathing slowly are important strategies to keep you from becoming reactive (Canter & Canter, 1993). The good old rule of walking away and counting to 10, or maybe 100, depending on the day, is still a good rule of thumb to keep from reacting to a child's behavior.

Proactive Discipline Ideas

Lavoie (1996a), Levine (2002), Rief (2005), Charles (2005), and other behavioral experts suggest some of the following strategies to support proactive rather than reactive behavior management:

- Anticipate problems and difficulties by preparing students for changes in routines, schedules, and testing.
- Help students deal with the anxiety that these changes cause by reassuring them that you understand how unsettling these changes are. Practice walking through what will happen, or use social stories to support the upcoming change.
- Help the students accept the responsibility for their behavior by helping them see and identify where they made wrong choices *after* they are no longer emotionally involved with the behavior. This direct instruction on good choice making will help the students the next time the opportunity occurs.
- Provide a token economy to reinforce appropriate behaviors. We like to be paid and recognized for the work that we do, and students like to be rewarded in a similar fashion. When providing a token, be sure to provide a social or verbal reinforcement as well.
- Verbally reinforce appropriate behavior whenever possible. A simple "Thank you for following directions," goes a long way in reinforcing appropriate behaviors. All students essentially want to please their teachers. When you recognize their attempts, they will be highly likely to continue trying to please you.
- Reward direction, not perfection. When you see students attempting to improve their behavior, it is important to recognize their efforts even

when the target behavior has not yet been perfectly achieved. Encouraging their attempts will increase the likelihood that they will continue to work toward the desired behavior.

- Review behavioral expectations prior to activities. Have students orally repeat directions back several times to ensure they have a clear understanding of the expectations.
- Provide classroom structure and routine that supports students with ADHD and other executive functioning weaknesses.

  - Provide a visual agenda.
  - Provide a warning signal for transitions.
  - Post four or five positively stated class rules (e.g., rather than "Don't rock your seat," the rule should be, "Keep all legs of the chair on the floor").
  - Have a routine for everything you do: for passing out paper, collecting paper, lining up, taking attendance, classroom movement, and so forth.
  - Provide fair consequences and enforce them with consistency.

Corrective Discipline

There are times when proactive discipline has not worked and corrective discipline must occur. These times include the need to stop a behavior for the sake of the instruction of your class, or the safety of the child and others around him or her. There are times when the corrective action can take place before the behavior has occurred. This is accomplished when you can recognize that a disruption is brewing. In a preschool setting, this often is a fight over a toy or a certain activity. Before letting the blowout occur, it might be good to distract one of the students with a different activity or toy, and when emotions are calmed, talk about ways to share and role play how to ask for a toy. Many of these same strategies can support all young learners in school settings:

- Distract or redirect the student from being disruptive; call on them to read, point to something on a map, or do a job like get a marker or erase the board.
- Flick the lights or ring a bell to signal "stop and listen." Sometimes this change of environment will stop the behavior.
- When disruptions begin, move closer to the student. This "proximity control" is sometimes enough to stop behavior without any verbal warnings or instruction.
- When a student begins to get involved in a disruption, sending them to a "nonpunitive exile" can be very effective. This may involve taking a note to the office or books to the library.

- Specifically telling students what you want them to do, not what you don't want them to do, will change behavior. Telling them to "Keep the crayons on the table" is a better directive than, "Don't throw the crayons." If students are "doing" something, they are less likely to misbehave.
- Keep busy hands "busy" by using fidget toys to help control motor activity. Waiting is difficult for students with ADHD. Even preschoolers often have to wait their turn and find this difficult. Having a toy they can play with in their hands gives them something to do while they wait. Fidgets can be small squishy toys or can simply be made by filling a high-quality latex balloon with sand or cornstarch.

Reasonable and Logical Consequences

If behavior needs to be stopped or misbehavior has occurred, appropriate consequences are required. ADHD is not an excuse for inappropriate behavior, and consistent behavioral expectations must be enforced. If consequences are necessary, it should be reasonable and logical (Wong & Wong, 2001). Reasonable consequences are ones that follow logically from the behavior rather than are arbitrarily imposed. The best logical consequences are those that teach students to choose between appropriate and inappropriate actions or responses. Logical consequences are related to the inappropriate behavior. For example, if the student colors all over the table, a logical consequence would involve the student cleaning the table, or if a student runs into the classroom, a logical consequence is making him or her go back and walk. When students see the logical connection between what they do and what happens to them, it helps them learn to choose between appropriate and inappropriate behavior (Wong & Wong, 2001). In short, the consequences reinforce the appropriate choice or behavior. Important rules for consequences are:

- Make sure that the consequences are immediate and definite. Students need to be clear on what the consequences are and should deal with the consequence as soon as possible. Consequences should not be put off for another day or time. If the consequence cannot be immediate, it should at least be definite (Lavoie, 1996a). For example, if washing the crayon off the tables would disrupt instruction, a clear message that the tables will be washed at recess makes the consequence definite.

- Made sure that the consequence is consistent and fits the inappropriate behavior. The consequence should always be related to a specific rule that is broken, so that the student clearly can see the connection between the consequence and their behavior.

- Time-out is an effective consequence if used appropriately. Time-out should not serve as an exile, but rather a place where a child who may have been receiving reinforcement from his or her peers for inappropriate behavior receives no reinforcement for the inappropriate behavior. With no audience, most inappropriate behaviors will stop. A good rule of thumb is a minute in time-out for each year of the child's age. A four-year-old should only be spending about four minutes in time-out when time-out is implemented appropriately (Lavoie, 1996a).

SUMMARY

So how do you keep children with ADHD and other difficult behaviors from driving you crazy? Hopefully these strategies and ideas will help you create a classroom environment that is built around a positive behavior philosophy in which the goal of each day is not so much compliance as it is the development of appropriate social skills and behaviors. As an effective teacher of young children, including those with ADHD, your dedication to teaching and respect for the diversity of your students will make your classroom one where all students feel safe enough to learn. Your ability to create a well-managed, organized classroom environment where behavioral expectations are clear and consistent will foster an environment in which all children are engaged and excited about learning. Your classroom will be a place where all children, including children with ADHD, will find a great beginning for their educational and emotional success.

How Do I Teach This Kid?   5

Classroom Strategies to Support All Learners

Teachers today are faced with the difficult tasks of trying to meet state, district, and program standards at every turn. They find that they are hard-pressed from every side to produce specific results for all children. While state and federal standards tell us as educators *what* we should teach, they do not dictate *how* we teach. The decisions about how you will teach *all* your students, including those with ADHD or other special needs, are left up to you, your expertise, and your professional knowledge as the teacher. We hope the suggestions found in this chapter will help you feel that you do have choices in how to make all students in your classroom successful.

CLASSROOM SUCCESS *IS* POSSIBLE

Can students with ADHD be successful in the classroom? Our answer is a resounding yes! We can look at some of the successful people who have struggled with ADHD and learning disabilities and yet have proven themselves successful in the world. Henry Winkler, Tom Cruise, Bill Hewlett, Bill Gates, Bruce Jenner, and Charles Schwab have all struggled with learning issues and are some of the most successful people in our country. The hidden disability did not keep them from attaining their goals. This chapter is written to help you, the educator, allow these students to reach their goals, whatever they may be.

If we were to interview the individuals mentioned previously, we would probably find that they each had a special teacher in their lives who allowed them to "show what they know" in some different way. These teachers understood their students' unique strengths and weaknesses and gave them alternate opportunities to show their mastery of the required academic tasks. These special teachers had the innate ability to adapt teaching strategies to meet the needs of their students. These teachers clearly understood the fairness principle and did not view adapting strategies as cheating or unfair. They did not think twice about re-reading questions to help a student with attention issues or allowing a student to answer test questions orally rather than in writing.

TREATING CHILDREN WITH ADHD FAIRLY

When teachers understand that students with ADHD often have difficulty with organizing their thinking and persisting through tedious tasks, they allow students to do only 15 of the 30 addition problems required for homework or to show their work on only 5 out of the 15 problems required. Some may ask, "Why would this not be considered 'cheating?'" When looking at the absolute fact that these students must cognitively struggle with bringing their thoughts to the task at hand and that homework takes them twice as long, it only makes it "fair" to give them half the work. It is not as if they will finish the 15 problems rather than the 30 in half the time; it will take equally as much or more time than a student without ADHD. There is nothing fair about having a 45-minute math homework assignment take three hours for a child with ADHD. "Leveling the playing field" should be one of the tools teachers use whenever they deem necessary to assist a student with ADHD to achieve success in the classroom.

DEFINING THE OBJECTIVE OF THE LESSON

Beyond the question of fairness, good teachers are able to glean from an assignment what the assignment is ultimately testing and allow the student with ADHD to meet the mastery of that standard in an alternative way. For example, a student who is learning how to regroup in addition might be assigned a worksheet in which the tens and ones must be assembled with manipulatives, then drawn or colored on a worksheet, and then solved using a vertical addition problem. For a child with ADHD, these multiple steps might prove to be too long and confusing. In this case, the teacher might allow the child with ADHD to show how to assemble the manipulatives and then solve the problem using the vertical addition problem and then allow the student to move on to problem solving, rather than continue with all three steps for all the problems provided.

Students with ADHD often resist having to show all the steps when they already know them and can move forward without having to show their work. They are often very bright and can "see" the answer, but have a difficult time breaking it organizationally into all its parts. They should not be penalized for their innate abilities to see the bigger picture and get the answer correct without showing their work. In this case, the teacher wants to know if the student can regroup, not work with manipulatives or re-create the example of manipulatives. If the student shows competence in the real objective, addition with regrouping, then the other steps can be eliminated.

The question that we as educators need to ask ourselves in looking at alternative strategies is: What is the objective of the lesson? What are the learning "destinations" for the students engaged in this lesson (Wiggins & McTighe, 1998)? What are the ways that this objective can be met? What is the evidence that will prove that the students have reached the goal? When teachers realize that there are truly a variety of ways that one objective can be measured and that this evidence can take on a variety of forms, students with learning differences and ADHD are more likely to be successful.

THE DIFFERENTIATED CLASSROOM

In the differentiated classroom, teachers recognize that students vary in the amount of background knowledge they have, their readiness to learn, their language skills, their learning preferences, and their interests. Teachers must respond to all these specific needs with a variety of instructional strategies. Teachers adjust their instructional strategies in the following areas: content, process, and product (Gregory & Chapman, 2007; Tomlinson, 2000, 2001).

Teachers who provide differentiation in the area of *content* provide multiple examples of how a student may meet one objective or standard, highlight the critical features that support meeting the objective, and provide the supporting background knowledge so that the student can relate the situation to his or her own experiences.

How the teacher differentiates during instruction to meet the specific needs of the student is referred to as the *process*. Teachers who differentiate in the instructional process provide information in multimedia formats with numerous supported opportunities for practice, and they employ strategies that will engage all learners, including students with ADHD. The outcome, or *product* for the differentiated classroom allows flexible models and variations of skill performance as well as numerous opportunities to demonstrate skills to show that students have met the objective. Differentiating gives the teacher the flexibility to create diverse assignments within a larger curriculum goal (Smutney & von Fremd, 2004).

Differentiation Strategies for Math and Literacy

Math

When differentiating the math curriculum for young students, the key to engagement and true learning comes when the teacher creates situations that inspire observation, reasoning, and imagination (Smutney & von Fremd, 2004). It is important to note that for young children, the concepts of math do not come out of textbooks, but actually are learned through their daily interactions with the world around them. Keep that in mind when teaching children.

Math will make all students more successful. In our current standards-driven age, assessment and instruction does lean heavily on paper-and-pencil tasks. For children with ADHD and other learning differences to be successful, the following accommodations should be provided:

- *Allow students the option of using manipulatives when needed.* Since math concepts are concrete, students need the option to use concrete objects to practice and discover math concepts. The opportunity to reinforce concepts with manipulatives is the perfect chance for them to learn to generalize the concrete concept to the symbolic math on their papers.

- *Allow students more space on worksheets to solve problems.* Many students with fine motor, organizational, or visual processing problems find it very difficult to fit all the required work into the space provided on the worksheet. The space is usually too small, and it is difficult to keep work aligned properly. Graph paper or dry erase boards provide the space and organization that students need to be able to successfully set up and solve problems.

- *Allow student to solve fewer problems.* It may take a child with ADHD several hours to finish the same amount of work that other students can do in 30 minutes. Reducing the number of problems is only fair when looking at the time it takes to complete the same number of problems.

- *Require student to "show work" on only a few problems.* Requiring students to "show their work" on every problem is too tedious for some students. Allow them to show how they solved one problem using the "show their work" process, and then let them show just the answers for the rest.

- *Provide students with worksheets with problems already written on them.* Students struggle significantly with copying problems accurately from a book or an overhead. If they copy the problem wrong, they have no chance of getting the answer correct. Providing a photo copy or adapted worksheet with the problems on it avoids this problem.

- *Provide immediate feedback to avoid the repeated application of an incorrect concept.* Do not wait until the student has solved a whole page of problems before providing feedback. If students only have three to five problems to solve, the teacher can monitor a few problems on each student's page as he or she passes through the room. Have students frequently show their work on a white board or go to the board to solve a problem, so that the teacher can quickly assess who does and does not understand the concepts.

- *Pair struggling students with a helping peer.* If students have poor decoding skills, pair them with a more capable reader who can provide kind, corrective support to help them with decoding of word problems.

Reading

When differentiating the language arts curriculum, it is of primary importance to become familiar with the prior knowledge and experiences that a child brings to the subject. You cannot expect a child who has had no experience with a hen to understand or make any meaning of the sentence, "The hen is in the pen." Good differentiated instruction will provide children with the background knowledge necessary to make sense of what they are decoding, otherwise decoding becomes a meaningless task that students do not enjoy. The child with ADHD will not have the sustained attention or interest in simply decoding sounds that lack any meaning. For young learners to obtain meaning from text, they must make connections between themselves and the written word. The teacher will have to model how to make these connections through the modeling of asking questions and encouraging the students to ask questions, relating what they are reading to real-life experiences, and learning to obtain meaning from the print in the environment around them.

The greatest struggle that students with ADHD have with reading is holding the sequence of story events together. They are often confused not because they can't read the text, but because of their struggle with comprehending the events in the story. To support student success in reading, some of the following strategies should be employed:

- *Teach how to paraphrase and summarize.* Students need to learn how to summarize and identify the important points in their own words. This can be taught efficiently by asking key comprehension questions during reading to help the student recognize how to glean the important information.

- *Use graphic organizers when possible.* Providing students with a graphic organizer that is filled in while they read will provide the direct instruction that they need to see how to identify the main characters, setting, and events. Modeling by the teacher on the overhead or board provides the kind of direct instruction needed to learn these specific content standards. Graphic organizers can also be used to sequence story events while reading and help students identify the main idea.

- *Allow highlighting of text passages.* To aid in comprehension, allowing the students to highlight key words or phrases will keep them more engaged while reading, but will also help them be able to answer questions or identify key points following the reading. Keeping a clear transparency over the text while the student reads and highlights will protect the book.

- *Preview vocabulary and lesson-specific concepts.* If students are to be engaged in what they are reading, they must understand the context and the vocabulary of the story. Spending deliberate daily time on vocabulary development is an important part of their future academic success. Vocabulary skills are the greatest predictor of academic success. Teachers should never shortchange students by not spending ample time ensuring that students have adequate vocabulary skills to understand a story. Vocabulary can be greatly enhanced by using picture books and trade books to help students be able to relate to the stories that they read.

- *Provide opportunities to read aloud.* Children with ADHD are engaged when they are involved. Allowing students to read aloud is one way to keep them involved. This does not always have to be reading in front of the class, but can involve reading to a partner or stuffed animal in the class. Reading fluency skills are built by having the opportunity to read aloud and can be achieved in a variety of ways that do not need to include waiting for a turn to read in front of the class.

- *Always discuss what is being read.* Before, during, and after each paragraph or section, the topic, the characters, and the vocabulary need to be discussed. It is this frequent discussion, relating the story to the children's own lives or experiences that brings reading alive and gives it meaning. Even wiggly children with ADHD love to hear and participate in good literature when they are supported and actively involved in understanding what is read.

Writing

Although the subject of developing writing skills will be discussed at length in the next chapter, the same principles of differentiation pertain to writing as they do in math and reading. Writing is an area in which the product or outcome of the lesson can look very different from child to child. In a differentiated classroom, all students are provided a menu of options to meet the specific objective or standard of the lesson. If, for instance, the objective is writing their first name, the menu of options might include writing in a sand tray, using markers on large paper, using markers on a dry erase board, using sidewalk chalk on the playground, using plastic or magnetic letters to write their name, or using playdough or Wicki Sticks to make the shapes of the letters of their name. This is not an exhaustive list, but gives you the idea that there are many more ways to show that students understand the order of the letters that make up their first name than a paper-and-pencil task.

Allowing only a paper-and-pencil task does not take into consideration the fact that the child may struggle with fine motor skills, may not be able to correctly hold and balance a pencil, may not simultaneously be able to hold the paper down with the other hand, or may not be able to form the shapes of the letters when written on smaller, lined paper. When this test of writing their name on a piece of lined paper is given to measure the objective of "writing their name," a number of skills are required that really have nothing to do with recognizing the order of the letters that represents their name. Often, a child with ADHD may not seem to be able to meet this objective, yet it has nothing to do with being able to remember the order of the letters for his or her name, but has more to do with the other skills required when trying to write on lined paper.

Differentiation may require some extra effort on the part of the teacher, but research has shown that students are more successful, especially in writing, when they are provided options that circumvent writing to show their knowledge (Tomlinson, 2001). Some of the easiest options available to most students should include being able to verbally respond rather than write if the objective is not related to a writing standard. Reading comprehension should not be limited by the ability or inability to write. Letting a student orally summarize a story is not "cheating," as the objective is determining if the student has comprehended the passage read, rather than his or her ability to write a paragraph that summarizes the story. Another quick and easy option is to allow the student to draw the sequence of story events that create a story summary if a one-on-one verbal summary is not possible.

Again, by providing students a differentiated classroom environment where all students have greater access to the specific concepts and skills taught by varying the level of difficulty and responding to specific interest and learning styles, all students, including students with ADHD, will find school enriching, exciting, and engaging.

MAKING APPROPRIATE ACCOMMODATIONS

Before Referral: Response to Intervention

Response to Intervention (RTI) is the practice of providing high-quality instruction and intervention matched to student need, which sounds much like differentiation, but it involves more intentional and frequent progress monitoring and child response data to make important educational decisions

(Batsche et al., 2005). RTI is a newly identified process described in the Individuals with Disabilities Education Act of 2004 (IDEA) for identifying students with learning disabilities. In an RTI model, all at-risk students are provided interventions early on, which research shows prevents some students from subsequently needing special education services. To qualify as learning disabled under this new model, a child would "fail to respond" to intensive interventions provided before a referral to special education. The lack of response to the interventions becomes part of the process in the identification of a learning disability, rather than a discrepancy between cognitive skills and academic achievement. This model seems to hold promise for those students who would benefit from early intervention services, rather than having to wait until a significant discrepancy between ability and achievement appears.

Children with ADHD are affected negatively because of diminished capacity to maintain attention and can be impaired in their ability to focus on basic curriculum development during the primary grades. The consequence, as they move up in grades, is that they may develop gaps in their learning. The RTI models are intended to prevent such gaps from widening and creating a situation in which the child will need special education services. Without early intervention, these gaps become especially problematic in upper grades, in which mastery or proficiency in basic curriculum is essential for academic success. When proficiency is poor, children with learning disabilities often feel like failures, and they are at risk for "giving up" during adolescence. They are at especially high risk for dropping out of school or not graduating under these conditions. While medications can clearly ameliorate the core symptoms of ADHD, there are no medications that specifically target learning disabilities. There are, however, a wide variety of educational techniques and strategies that can be implemented to develop, strengthen, or compensate for weaknesses associated with many kinds of learning disabilities.

Professionals have generally held off formal testing for specific learning disabilities until a child is in the second or third grade. Younger school-age children often did not qualify for special education placement under the former specific learning disabled criteria of "significant discrepancy" because they did not show a large enough gap between their IQ and achievement test scores. With the inception of the RTI model, students should be able to access academic interventions early on and will not have to "wait to fail" before they can receive academic help.

Accommodations Under Section 504

Children who have a diagnosis of ADHD but who do not qualify for special education services may be entitled to accommodations and modifications under Section 504 of the Rehabilitation Act of 1973. It is important to keep in mind that not all children with ADHD are in fact in need of accommodations. According to the law, the disorder must "substantially limit a major life activity, including...learning" (Section 504, 34 C.F.R. § 104.3[j][1][ii]). These accommodations provide children with ADHD an

> equal opportunity to obtain the same results, to gain the same benefit or to reach the same level of achievement. These aids or benefits are not required to produce the identical result, or level of achievement for both students with disabilities and those without. (Section 504 34 C.F.R.§ 104.33[b][1])

Students with 504 plans are allowed accommodations for daily class work as well as for all standardized testing.

This broad civil rights law protects the rights of individuals with handicaps in programs that receive federal financial assistance and ensures that any person with a disability has the same rights and opportunities that his or her nondisabled peers have. A Section 504 plan is not a special education document and is not the responsibility of the special education staff at the school site, although special educators are often called on to provide suggestions and support for the 504 plan. They may also be involved in providing some of the accommodations that require a separate place to work or extra time for assignments.

Determining Which Accommodations Will Work

How do you go about determining what strategies or accommodations might work for your students? Dr. Diana Browning Wright (2003) uses the following strategies and steps in determining just how and when to make changes to or make accommodations for students with ADHD or learning differences. She starts with the following questions to determine what changes are necessary:

- *Can the child participate successfully in this activity just like the other students?* If, from previous experience with the child, it is determined that no changes or accommodations are necessary, then nothing special needs to be done.
- *Can classroom organizational changes and instructional practice benefit all students?* If lessons and activities are designed so that they would increase the participation, motivation, task completion, and quality of work of all students, the student with ADHD will also benefit.

- *Can the child with ADHD participate with additional environmental accommodations?* These adaptations might include support from additional peers, teachers, and adults, or might include a different work environment or space in the classroom.
- *Can the student participate with input or output adaptations?* Providing graphic organizers, pre-teaching, practice, and visual support are adaptations that support the student's understanding of the instruction. Allowing for differentiated responses, such as drawing or verbalizing, assists in allowing the student to demonstrate what was learned.
- *Can the student learn better and demonstrate that knowledge with changes in time allotted for work or testing?* Allowing the student extra time or the opportunity to redo an assignment are appropriate adaptations for students with ADHD.
- *Can the student master the material without completing all the work assigned?* Can the quantity be reduced and the student still show competence? This adaptation allows the student to demonstrate the standard even though a smaller quantity of work is produced.
- *Can the student master the material with a reduction in difficulty of material presented?* This adaptation would allow the child the opportunity to meet the essential standard with a reduction of task difficulty. For example, if the standard is sentence writing, this adaptation would allow the student to write only a sentence to meet the requirement rather than several sentences in a paragraph.

Common Adaptations and Accommodations

The most common and easiest-to-use curricular adaptations involve simply adapting the number of items that the student must complete or adapting the time allotted to complete a task. Others include adapting the way instruction is delivered. For example, a teacher might use a visual aid such as an overhead projector, involve the students in concrete, hands-on examples, or give the class clear, sequenced directions. Each of these methods works for everyone in the class, but they are particularly helpful for students with attention difficulties.

Another very helpful adaptation is to allow certain students to respond differently to the instruction. As mentioned earlier, this might include verbal responses or the opportunity show knowledge with hands-on or visual activities rather than writing. For some students, an appropriate adaptation would be to increase the amount of personal assistance. This assistance could be provided by a peer buddy, a teaching assistant, a peer tutor, or a cross-age tutor. Table 5.1 lists specific accommodations and what they entail.

Table 5.1   Accommodations for Children With Learning Disabilities

Accommodation	What It Involves
Flexible scheduling	• Extended time for tests and assignments • Modified duration of tests (breaks during test, test scheduled over several sessions or days)
Flexible setting	• Individual administration of a test or assignment • Small-group administration of a test or assignment • Adaptive or special equipment, such as the use of a computer or Alpha Smart
Adapted test or assignment format	• Reduced number of test items per page, or the ability to circle test answers on test documents rather than the "bubble in" sheets
Adapted directions	• Rewriting or rewording test directions • Repeated test directions or prompts • Emphasizing key words or work patterns in directions • Reading of standard directions to the student
Aids to interpret or respond to test items	• An auditory tape to record answers, oral responses • A word processor, computer, or Alpha Smart to record non-oral responses • Teacher cues to maintain on task behavior, including allowing student to read test and assignment questions out loud • A test booklet in which responses can be directly recorded

Other classroom accommodations can include:

Instructional

- Provide an overview of the lesson before starting to focus student's thinking.
- Schedule frequent checks for understanding to ensure that student has been following along, and redirecting if necessary.
- Give intermittent and frequent breaks to move around and interact with others.

- Use specific daily routines, agendas, and organizational strategies.
- Increase the amount of time allowed to complete all assignments and tests.
- Plan short work periods with frequent breaks or change of tasks.
- Give students specific tasks to perform within a specific time period.
- Allow students "nonpunitive exile" by asking them to run an errand or take a walk when getting frustrated or physically restless.
- Allow student to doodle constructively while listening to teacher present information.

Environmental

- Use a quiet place to work or a barrier between desks.
- Use a seat in front of the class or seat in back of the class depending on distractibility level.
- Provide another optional desk to move to when student needs to move to attend better.
- Provide a seat away from high-traffic areas and distracters like the pencil sharpener, drinking fountain, coat hooks, heater, air conditioners, and windows.
- Use carpet squares or hula hoops as well as tape markers on the floor to signify a specific sitting place when seated on the floor.
- Allow an empty seat next to student if possible for excessive movement.
- Store materials away from the desk or out of reach to alleviate distractions.
- Have designated quiet transition times between recess and other noisy activities.
- Turn off lights to calm students during transitions from noisy activities.
- Be open, flexible, and willing to make changes in seating when needed.

Informational

- Avoid large amounts of written work including classwork and homework. Allow for shortened assignments or the use of a computer or Alpha Smart for written work including daily spelling and grammar assignments.
- Encourage the use of the writing method that is most comfortable: cursive or manuscript.
- Avoid having students copy from the board or overhead. If copying is required, provide a near-point sample, have a note taker, or have the teacher provide a copy.
- Avoid clutter and crowded worksheets, desk space, and classroom space.
- Give the student time during the week to clear out his or her desk and to organize materials with the support of the teacher.

- Allow the student to keep all assignments in a spiral notebook, to lessen the chance of lost work.

Homework

- Make arrangements for homework to reach home with clear, concise directions with options to check a homework hotline where assignments can be checked by phone or a homework study buddy in the same class who can be called for further clarification. Use the option to do homework on a computer and e-mail finished assignments to teachers.
- Reduce the number of problems to solve or questions to answer.
- Use visual responses such as pictures rather than written responses.
- Don't require students to answer questions in complete sentences.
- Allow assignments to be completed on a computer and e-mailed to the teacher.
- Allow extra time for all assignments—due on Monday following the Friday due date.
- Don't require students to show work for all math problems solved.
- Use graph paper to help with math organization.
- Have math problems provided by teacher rather than student copying problems from a book (Saxon math adaptations).
- Have parents or caregivers "scribe" responses to questions.
- Use graphic organizers for written assignments and book reports.
- Use computerized study guides.
- Provide access to a homework hotline or Web site with homework assignments posted.
- Provide access to a study buddy to help with directions and explanation of assignments.
- Have support of a nonfamily member as a tutor to help with math homework.
- Provide access to afterschool homework supplemental services and support.
- Provide specific reminders both verbally and visually to turn in homework that has been completed.

BEYOND ACCOMMODATIONS AND INTERVENTIONS: THE SPECIAL EDUCATION REFERRAL

Children with mild ADHD can usually pass through kindergarten, first grade, and the beginning of second grade before their inattention, gross motor activity, and poor fine motor skills bring them to the attention of the school's student study team or student success team. By the second half of second grade, much more independent work in all academic areas is required. Students with ADHD will find it difficult to meet these requirements, and teachers begin to become concerned at the child's assumed lack of ability. Feeling the need for support from others on how to best teach this child, the teacher calls a meeting. This meeting includes his or her peers, an administrator, and school experts, including a school psychologist and special educators to brainstorm strategies to support the student's success in his or her own classroom. Potential strategies are identified, and the teacher and student work on these strategies for a prescribed period of time. If the strategies prove unsuccessful, another meeting is called, and the team again looks at possible ways to help the student meet his or her potential and be successful in the classroom. Usually, the option discussed at this point is special education assessment to determine if the child has a specific learning disability.

LEARNING DISABILITIES

Experts estimate that 10% to 40% of children with ADHD have associated learning disorders that meet the criteria for a specific learning disability (Batshaw, 2002). Typically, children with ADHD and learning disabilities exhibit academic underachievement with the most difficulty with reading and written language. Affected children also have a high incidence of central auditory processing disorders and visual-motor functioning problems, which affect all aspects of classroom performance. Many children with ADHD qualify for special education services due to the presence of a comorbid identified specific learning disability.

   In the past, for a child to qualify as "learning disabled," the federal IDEA specified that the student had to be achieving at a level significantly lower than what is expected for his or her age and show a "significant discrepancy" between his or her ability and achievement. This would be reflected in a significant difference between cognitive skills and an academic achievement area on a standardized measurement of achievement. A learning disability was said to exist when this discrepancy between a child's cognitive ability (IQ) and academic achievement was large enough. When IDEA was reauthorized in 2004, the proposed regulations changed this requirement. The IDEA 2004 regulations now allow states to discontinue the use of the discrepancy model in lieu of an RTI model.

OTHER HEALTH IMPAIRED

Although there is a comorbidity of learning disability that often affects children diagnosed with ADHD, not all children who have ADHD who are tested qualify for special education services under the label of "specific learning disability." A child who is diagnosed with ADHD and is significantly impacted in all academic areas may qualify for special education services under the Federal Handicapping Condition of Other Health Impaired. This is not a common designation for most students who are only mildly affected by ADHD and is usually reserved for those children who do not respond to medication and behavioral therapy and need extra daily support through special education services provided by the school in an individualized education plan to successfully make educational progress.

SUMMARY

With the support of flexible classroom teachers, even young children with ADHD can be successful with the academic skills that they are required to master. When teachers understand that accommodations and modifications support the learning of children with ADHD, student success, motivation, and subsequent self-esteem will improve. When the unique qualities and gifts that these children present are clearly understood, classroom success is definitely attainable. We hope that the strategies provided in this chapter will help you in allowing the students that you encounter with ADHD to be successful in your classroom.

Why Is Writing So Hard?

6

Specific Strategies to Develop Writing Skills

W hen given a writing assignment, a child with ADHD will be observed doing any number of behaviors other than writing. This might include sharpening a pencil numerous times, walking to the trash to clean out the sharpener, making a trip to the drinking fountain, making a trip to get another clean sheet of paper, and then furiously searching the backpack for a writing instrument. All of these behaviors that are annoying to the teacher and others around him are really an attempt by this child to avoid a task that is as monumental as climbing Mount Everest is to us.

WHY WRITING IS SO HARD

The greatest academic difficulties that we see with students with ADHD are related to the area of writing. Almost all academic areas require students to prove their knowledge in content matter through responding in writing. Students who have weak writing skills rarely do well in their classes even when they have strong content knowledge. These students struggle due to the need for strong executive functioning skills to organize thoughts in a sequential manner. They also need the ability to capture those thoughts on paper before the thoughts fleetingly disappear. Students with ADHD are rarely successful in this area without scaffolding and specific support. For the young child with ADHD, making the connection between the symbols of the letters and the sounds and words that children speak is a very abstract connection. The concept that the written word is symbolic of the spoken word is a difficult one to teach. Establishing the relationship between symbols and the words we speak are the very first steps to writing proficiency.

TEACHING EARLY WRITING

Using Pictures

For early learners, the concept that words can be conveyed through visual means should begin with pictures, as even preschoolers have "read" picture books and have an understanding that pictures can convey a symbolic meaning and message. One of the most concrete ways to teach these concepts was shared during a lecture on "Optimal Learning Environments," a program to support English-language learners with special needs (Ruiz, 1997). The strategy has proven useful to teach the concept of symbols representing written language.

As suggested by Dr. Nadine Ruiz (1997), all writers fall along a spectrum of developing skills. To convey the idea that symbols communicate meaning, a drawing is shared with two heads facing each other with their mouths open (see Figure 6.1). This can easily be "decoded" as two girls talking. Even most young preschoolers would be able to interpret this written message. As students move toward developing writing skills, next we might see the two "talking" girls with a string of letters underneath that "tell" the story, although the letters may not have any sound-symbol relationship. However, students at this developmental level realize that letters can tell a story, and students will include them and miscellaneous creative marks to show "writing." As students further progress developmentally in the area of writing, the picture of the two girls remains with letter strings that show some sound-symbol relationships. For example, they might have "grlstlk" as their "story" under the picture. As they develop further, the letter strings will grow more phonetic and will include some sight words. For example, the sentence might now look like, "thegirlstalk" or might even include correct spacing, "the girls talk." Of course, as they progress, students will learn English-language conventions and ultimately the sentence will look like, "The girls are talking," with correct syntax, punctuation, capitalization, and tense agreement.

The reason we have spent so much time on this idea is that all students will go through these stages. If both students and teachers understand that each child's "writing" may look different, but still is considered writing, students feel more successful and teachers are less frustrated with what they may perceive as a lack of writing skills when the student might only be producing letter strings. Just as we don't get frustrated when a child crawls before walking, we should see letter strings as the crawling stage of the writing process.

Figure 6.1   Example of the Developmental Writing Process

SOURCE: Silvia L. DeRuvo.

Modeling

Some may ask, "Well, how do children learn the new skills that bring them closer to the correct spelling and sentence structure?" The answer is through *modeling*. Just as their parents modeled how to get dressed, eat foods, and communicate, children learn to write through modeling. When the student draws the two girls and writes a string of letters, the teacher responds in writing interactively with a response to their writing such as, "What are the girls talking about?" In this written response, students begin to make the connection between the symbols /g/ /i/ /r/ /l/ and the two heads that have represented the two girls (see Figure 6.1). Modeling the correct syntax, spelling, punctuation, and capitalization will provide the models that the students need to develop along the writing continuum.

Writing Prompts

Journal Writing

When this opportunity to model writing is interwoven into all curricular activities, the development of writing skills improves, especially with the use of journal writing. The positive effect of using journals in the classroom has been noted by many teachers. "Journal writing or free writing gets them used to putting words on paper," shared one teacher. Another teacher shared, "I see more daily growth in journal writing because it comes from the heart, is not corrected, and is only shared if the child chooses to share it." Indeed, journal writing is a powerful tool for beginning writers to develop their skills (Fink-Chorzempka, Graham, & Harris, 2005).

Individual Stories

Once students have developed the concept that the spoken word can be conveyed through the printed word, more specific writing tasks can be developed. Again, modeling continues to be the key for young learners, especially those with ADHD. Whole-group stories or a "student of the day" story is a way to continue to develop these concepts. In many classrooms, a student is chosen each day to be the "student of the day" or, as one school proclaimed these students, "wonderful" for the day. This practice is not only great for building self-esteem, it also allows the students an opportunity to get to know each other better. Usually at a circle time, the chosen students have the opportunity to share about themselves, and this is put into a story about them. The teacher writes the information on a large piece of chart paper, having the group as a whole help with the spelling, capitalization, and punctuation. Information might include the child's name, birth date, favorite color, pets, family information, and so forth. As students develop writing skills throughout the school year, the student (rather than the teacher) can eventually do the writing on the chart paper.

Class Stories

Class stories are similar in that the students give input and help the teacher with spelling and conventions, and the teacher models either on chart paper or on the overhead. For students in the elementary grades, the interview process can be used, in which the classmates develop the questions for a student on a specific topic chosen by the "author"—the interviewee. The responses are initially recorded as answers to questions. The teacher then models, with student support, the transition of the answers to a real paragraph, modeling the organization and sequencing process necessary for paragraph writing. These stories can then be retyped by the student, illustrated, and put into a class book of original stories.

The Stuffed Animal

Another frequently used writing prompt is the use of a class stuffed animal that goes home with one child each night. The next day, the child returns with the stuffed animal and tells about the adventures. In our case, Bingo, the stuffed dog, took many travels around our small town. Each morning, Bingo would return to be the subject of the daily journal entry (see Figure 6.2). The writing again was modeled by the teacher as the students practiced the oral language skills of asking the student who took Bingo home what adventures he or she had had that evening. Students practiced how to develop oral questions and how to answer in complete sentences and then helped the teacher with how to write those complete sentences into a journal entry. Bingo never left town, but he had some wonderful times in the grocery store, local park, and in the neighborhood. There is always the chance that Bingo could get lost (which did happen), but a replacement Bingo was quickly adopted and so continued the daily tradition of sharing his adventures. Crisis averted!

Flat Stanley

For older students in the primary grades, a way to develop this concept even further and to provide students another reason to write is the "Flat Stanley Project." In *Flat Stanley*, written by Jeff Brown, Stanley becomes flat when a bulletin board falls on him, making him flat enough to travel in an

Figure 6.2   The Stuffed Animal Story

SOURCE: Fred DeRuvo. Used by permission

envelope. The project involves journal writing and the practice of sending a "Flat Stanley" in the mail to relatives or friends in other parts of the country for adventures to be shared with them. These relatives are instructed to take Flat Stanley on local adventures, which could include simple things like spending a work day with someone or going to local attractions. The relatives or friends are instructed to take pictures of Flat Stanley in these places and then share the information in a letter or postcard. Some projects include entire classes exchanging Stanleys in different states and chronicling their adventures in journals. Once the students have Stanley back, they write stories about Stanley's journeys and adventures. Again, students have the opportunity to take models of written language from the letters and postcards as a scaffold and turn them into paragraphs with teacher support if necessary. (For more information about the Flat Stanley Project, visit http://flatstanley.enoreo.on.ca/.)

ANALYZING WRITING TASKS

When the writing tasks are analyzed, teachers need to recognize that there really are numerous skills necessary for what most of us consider writing, which is conveying spoken word into the written word. However, a skill that hampers many children with ADHD is the ability to form the letters needed to do the writing. The difficulties with fine motor skills lead to reluctant writers even if they have the concepts and ideas to write. According to Dr. Mel Levine (2002), expert on children with learning differences:

> Most obviously, some of the most complex muscular manipulations are demanded for writing. As we shall see, there are countless students with good ideas whose fingers just can't keep pace with their thinking, as a result of which they come to despise and avoid writing. (p. 171)

The experts do agree that it is appropriate to circumvent the student's difficulty with writing by allowing children to dictate their compositions or write with a keyboard like an Alpha Smart (Fink-Chorzempka et al., 2005). Bypassing writing and allowing the child to use other modalities and direct assistance from others is more beneficial than forcing a child with poor fine motor skills to produce volumes of writing.

Tracing

For very young children, practice in letter formation is important, as the ability to write is important, but this skill should not be required for all written assignments. Young children can learn the letter shapes simply by tracing them on top of a highlighted example on paper that is enlarged and has extra space between lines. This is a great way to teach the order of the letters of their name and the formation of the letters to write their names. They can also trace short stories, providing they are indeed short and not too long.

Copying

Copying is another option, but it is often very tedious and difficult for a child with attention issues, especially when having to copy from the board or overhead. In observing these children, you will find that they do not hold a cluster of letters in their visual memory as most of us do, but rather, due to poor planning, copy letter by letter. This process of looking up, finding one letter, remembering it, finding their place on their paper, writing the letter, then looking up again, finding the next letter, and repeating the process is one that most students with a great attention span would not want to do. Talk about tedious! If copying is necessary, students need a near-point sample, so that they can more quickly and easily find the letter that they are looking for without having to look up at the board so frequently.

There are numerous strategies to help students with copying or note taking from the board or overhead. Teachers can simply provide the students with a copy of the notes for them to follow along. They can be taught to use a highlighter to highlight key words and to ensure that they are following along. Teachers can also use the "cloze sentence" technique, in which the student has most of the information provided by the teacher, but key words are missing. The student only copies these key words from the overhead or the board as they are discussed by the class.

Assistance From Note Takers and Recorders

If the teacher is unable to provide the notes, another student can be chosen as a note taker, and the child who has difficulty with copying can obtain a photocopy of the notes from the note taker. Another option is to have the note taker use No Carbon Required (NCR) paper and give the second copy of the notes to the student with special needs (Rief, 1998). Students with ADHD might also need the accommodation of taping class discussions to be listened to at another time, to ensure that they have all the notes needed if they have attempted to copy them themselves. For students with ADHD, simultaneous processing is difficult, which makes note taking so difficult for them. Students struggle with writing, listening, and processing the information at the same time. If they are allowed just to listen while others take notes, or if they are allowed to tape the information while they write, they will more likely grasp and retain the important information.

Forming Letters

Learning how to form letters or develop appropriate handwriting skills does create a challenge for students with ADHD who have fine motor weakness and difficulty with hand-eye coordination (Lougy & Rosenthal, 2002). The program "Handwriting Without Tears" provides excellent developmental strategies to support children's poor motor planning and develop the prerequisite skills necessary for appropriate handwriting skills. The program takes into consideration the process of developing fine motor skills and, ultimately, good handwriting skills. For program information and training, we encourage you to visit the Web site, http://www.hwtears.com.

SCAFFOLDS FOR WRITING SUCCESS

The Writing Process

Once students are able to form letters and have a clear understanding of the connection between the spoken and written word, the true development of the writing process can occur. We usually see this process broken down into several steps that often include:

- brainstorming
- prewriting
- writing
- writing paragraphs
- editing
- creating a final draft

Although these may work for most students, for students with ADHD, there is not enough structure in each step to produce writing success. These students need support or scaffolds from one step to the next. Again, they will also need modeling of each scaffold before we can expect them to use a scaffold independently to support their own writing. The following sections demonstrate scaffolding within and modeling of the steps listed here.

Brainstorming

The brainstorming process is integral to the development of writing skills. In brainstorming, students are encouraged to share many ideas or words related to the topic that they will be writing about. The teacher accepts all ideas shared and writes them down for later reference. Again, the concept of verbal-to-print change is reinforced as the teacher writes students' verbal ideas down on paper. The teacher can use this opportunity to work on specific spelling skills or sound-symbol association skills as he or she has the class help him or her get the ideas on paper. For instance, if the story is going to be about an airplane ride and a student wants the word *jet* to be part of the list, the teacher may ask what letter the word starts with, what it ends with, or what vowel is in the middle, depending on the level of the class and concepts previously taught. A teacher can even take this further and ask what other words rhyme with *jet* or begin with the same beginning or ending letter.

Once this list has been developed, it can be used as a reference for spelling when students begin to work on their own writing, but it can and should also be used as a tool for letter and word recognition. The teacher can ask the students to come up to the chart and identify words that begin with a specific letter, or end with that target letter. He or she can also have students find words that have target vowel sounds, digraphs, or specific word families. Students might also work in teams to copy on the board or on small dry erase boards words from the brainstormed list that begin or end with a target letter or have a specific vowel family. Writing on the board is a tremendous tool to use to help students develop fine motor skills, as the large body movements needed for writing on the board are the prerequisite skills needed to eventually be successful with writing on lined paper. Any time the child has practice in interacting with the written word, stronger reading skills are developed. The opportunity for the child with ADHD to get up and identify words on the chart will help hold his attention and will allow him the movement he needs to be successful.

Teachers should not make the mistake of creating a wonderful rich word list and then leaving it alone. This list is a great teaching tool and can be used for days to reinforce sight words, letter sounds, and word families. As the students become more familiar with the words on the chart, they will be more likely to be able to identify the words that they need when they begin to write. They will recognize more of them due to the practice they received prior to writing. These prewriting strategies may seem time consuming, but they are strategies that strongly support reading and writing skills for all students, especially those with ADHD.

Prewriting

This brainstorming scaffold leads to the next step, which is the prewriting process. Beginning writers can use these now-familiar words in sentence frames. For more adept writers, these words can be used in graphic organizers to create a story outline or structure. Beginning writers are not yet ready to write sentences independently. This is often the mistake that is made, and both students and teachers are frustrated by the student's inability to write a complete sentence after a simple brainstorming task. Students who experience difficulty with writing need more practice as an appropriate adaptation to support their writing skills (Fink-Chorzempka et al., 2005).

Sentence Frames. Students need the support of beginning sentence writing with a sentence frame such as: "On my plane ride, I saw _____. The plane ride felt _____." (See Figure 6.3.) These frames can be easily created in a slot chart so that students have the opportunity to now use the familiar words in the brainstorm chart to finish their thoughts and complete their sentences. You may recognize that quite a bit of modeling of syntax, spelling, and conventions is still being provided in this "independent" writing lesson.

One way to take this frame writing a step further is to turn this into a book that students can independently "read." This book can easily be constructed from sentence strips that are cut into 12-inch lengths. These lengths are folded in half at the six-inch mark and bound with a rubber band. The three- to four-sentence strips make a six- to eight-page book that can now hold several sentence frames related to the topic creating students' own story (see Figure 6.4).

Figure 6.3   Writing Scaffold in Slot Chart

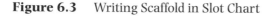

SOURCE: Fred DeRuvo.

Figure 6.4   Sentence Strip Book

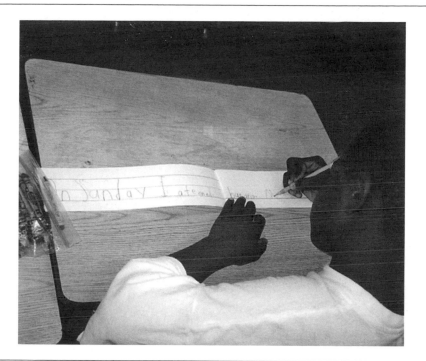

SOURCE: Silvia L. DeRuvo.

If students struggle with copying the words from the brainstorm chart, these words can be put on index cards so that the students can go up to the slot chart and take out the words that they need to finish their story. This again provides the opportunity for the child with ADHD to move during a lesson and gives him or her the opportunity to copy the words needed from a near-point sample. Students can also have the teacher or aide copy in highlighter the words that they need, and the students can trace over them. Once the words are all written, of course the fun part is illustrating the sentence on the space that is left on the sentence strip. The key is that students feel supported in their attempts to write and that—no matter what—they will find success in this type of activity. The importance of motivating struggling writers is as vital as providing adaptations. "Encouragement and praise was a necessary adaptation for struggling writers" (Fink-Chorzempka et al., 2005, p. 65). If we show students that writing is enjoyable, rather than excruciating, they will learn to love to write.

As beginning writers move toward independent writing, they will initially start with copying a section of text and then adding their own words as discussed previously with sentence frames. This essential practice before writing is important before expecting students to write independently. Further practice with manipulating words in the sentence strip is needed prior to expecting students, especially students with ADHD and learning disabilities, to begin to put words into sentence formats on their own. To provide this practice, a complete sentence that they are familiar with can be provided in the slot chart.

The sentences might be about the airplane ride from the sentence strip book, "On my plane ride, I saw a white cloud." Students practice reading this sentence as the teacher points to each word. Students make the association between the letters and the words that are being read. Students then become actively engaged by first coming up to the slot chart and identifying the words in order as the other students read them. This interactive process keeps the student with ADHD engaged and moving around during the lesson. After students can identify the words in order, the teacher then has the students identify the target words out of order. For example, he might ask students to first identify *ride* and then *on* and then *cloud*. Once students have had numerous opportunities to practice words out of order, the sentence strip should be cut up, and students should be given the words on the cut-up strip to put into the slot chart in correct order. The teacher would direct the student with the word *on* to put it in the slot chart in the correct place and so on until the complete sentence is in place. This again allows numerous students to move around and actively be involved in the reading and writing process. This manipulating of the written word teaches the concepts that sentences are made up of words and when these words are put together in a certain order, they tell a thought.

If we as teachers ask students prior to all this prewriting practice to write sentences, they become frustrated and refuse to follow directions and complete the task. This usually leads to some sort of punitive punishment and a further lowering of the child with ADHD's self-esteem. This would be like asking someone with no knowledge of cars to fix his or her own carburetor—the person wouldn't know where to find it, let alone know how to fix it! These students feel the same bewilderment and frustration in asking them to deal with letters that make words that are supposed to be put together to make sense, but there is not enough practice to support this independent task. Students with ADHD who have limited persistence and attention span will often find such a request meaningless and will find that their thoughts have drifted to something that does make sense, is real, and relates to their own life. This often looks like willful disobedience when they are found playing with a toy or getting up to do a task that might be familiar, like talking to another student or choosing an activity that is not appropriate for a writing period.

Writing

To develop independent writing skills from such prewriting lessons, students must have many opportunities to practice and manipulate words.

This allows them to learn correct word order or syntax. When they get to practice moving word cards around on their own, they discover that only the correct word, or syntax, makes sense. For young children, this makes a great writing center as the sets of word cards could be provided for each of the four to five students who use the center. Students can rotate through the centers and practice putting several sentences together from a set of word cards. With this type of intensive prewriting practice, students who are ready to take the step to independent writing will have less confusion and less frustration due to their gained knowledge of correct word order, capitalization, and punctuation that has been modeled through all of these activities. Also, practice with manipulating words that are frequently used helps students visually identify the words to improve reading skills. In addition, as students develop a visual memory for these words, they will also improve their spelling skills, a difficulty common to students with ADHD. Providing a "word wall" also becomes an invaluable tool for those moments when students are not able to access the correct spelling of the word from memory. This tool helps them to know that there is another way to figure out the spelling of the word rather than guessing.

Writing Paragraphs

For preschool and kindergarten teachers, having their students achieve independent sentence writing makes these students advanced or proficient based on most state standards. However, by the time students are in second or third grade, most are expected to be able to write paragraphs independently with a proper introductory sentence, three supporting sentences, and a conclusion sentence. Again, just telling a student about this structure and providing a graphic organizer with these headings is not enough. No real writing is going to occur, and you will probably see less-than-perfect behavior or compliance. The child with ADHD may be seen as being defiant for not using the graphic organizer provided to create the perfect paragraph. As with independent sentence writing skills, independent paragraph writing skills also need to be taught using sentence frames and specific scaffolds to help students practice what it means to write a paragraph.

Students must begin the process with brainstorming words or ideas related to the topic. Here again, the teacher or a scribe from the class writes the words on an overhead or large piece of paper. 3M sticky chart paper is great to use, as it can be moved around the room so it can be brought closer to the child with attention issues or copying problems. It can be stored out of the way by being stuck to the back of the door or another out-of-the-way place until it is needed for writing time again the next day. In this way, students who might be writing during independent work time can pull out the correct chart, stick it up, and use it to support their writing without interrupting the teacher or having to access the board or turn on the overhead. Different charts can also be used for different topics for each paragraph. For example, if students are writing three paragraphs on what they learned about rabbits from their reading book, each chart can be headed with a topic for each paragraph. As students brainstorm, they can tell the teacher or the scribes which category their idea should go in. This is great practice for categorization, which is often a weakness for children with ADHD and learning disabilities.

It is after the brainstorming that the graphic organizers come into play. If students have been provided the scaffold of a chart that is labeled with a specific category, like "what rabbits eat" and the facts have been brainstormed on that chart, students can then choose from that chart what they want to write about in their paragraph pertaining to that topic. If the class has chosen the ideas, "what rabbits look like," "what rabbits eat," and "where rabbits live," students can write these topics on their own graphic organizer and then copy the word or words that they want to use to write their own sentences on the topic. For novice writers, these topics can be provided for the students on the organizer itself by the teacher.

Now the question that often arises at this point is, "Aren't they just copying?" Yes, they are copying the organization of thoughts provided by the graphic organizer, *but* they will be writing sentences independently based on the organization of these thoughts. Remember, it is not that children with ADHD cannot write or do not have thoughts that they can put in writing. The opposite is usually true. They usually have so many thoughts, they can't catch and organize them to be able to put them into meaningful sentences. The brainstorming and categorizing process helps them get organized enough to put their thoughts into meaningful order. Most students can move forward independently when using a graphic organizer similar to the one shown in Figure 6.5.

Introductory and Concluding Sentences. The two most troubling sentences in the paragraph remain to be discussed. The introductory and concluding sentences will continue to confuse students who have organization problems.

Two ways to support students in determining what to write about in the introductory sentence is to look at the content of the supporting sentences and then, from the information derived from those sentences, determine what the paragraph is about. For example, a paragraph that has three sentences that tell what rabbits look like, what they eat, and where they live might give the student the idea that the paragraph is about rabbits and some interesting facts about rabbits. An introductory sentence can then be derived from these facts. For example, the student might decide to write an introductory sentence, such

Figure 6.5   Graphic Organizer

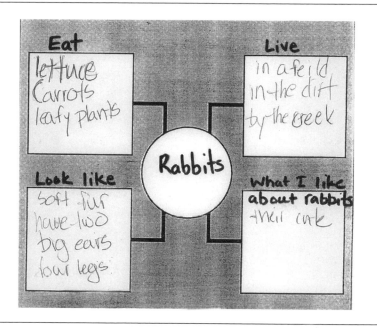

as "Rabbits are interesting animals," or "I know a lot about rabbits," then give the three facts he or she has learned. Determining the introduction based on the facts given in the writing helps the student recognize the connection between the introduction and supporting sentence. A strategy recommended by Diana Browning Wright (2003) includes having students practice with a series of sentences on sentence strips of index cards that contain a main topic sentence and three supporting statements as well as concluding sentences. Students practice recognizing which type of sentence each card has and then put the paragraph in the correct order by manipulating the cards or strips before any writing occurs (Browning Wright, 2003).

Another strategy to use when students are stuck is to simply provide introductory sentence phrases on the word wall to help in those moments when the words just won't flow. Hopefully the prompts in Form 6.1 will help students come up with similar topic sentence or concluding sentence ideas.

Most students with ADHD can be successful with appropriate modeling, practice, and the use of meaningful graphic organizers. A variety of graphic organizers that you can print out and use right away are available on the Internet; to find them, do a Google search using the phrase "graphic organizers."

A few students will still find the step from graphic organizer to written sentences too difficult to make. Most of these students do not lack ability, but due to inappropriate teaching strategies, lack of practice, and a lot of

Form 6.1   Introductory and Concluding Sentence Samples

Introductory Sentence Examples

I believe _____ .

What do you know about _____ ?

Have you ever seen a _____ ?

Let me tell you about _____ .

There are many different things _____ .

There are many different kinds _____ .

I find _____ very interesting.

Concluding Sentence Examples

I think _____ .

In my opinion _____ .

I believe _____ .

In conclusion _____ .

I hope you agree _____ .

After all, _____ ?

---

frustration, these students lack the self-confidence to try to put a paragraph together independently. They struggle with taking the ideas that they have copied onto the graphic organizer to the written page. These few students need the continued scaffold of sentence frames in the paragraph format (see Form 6.2).

From these examples, you can see that the student is again supported with the structure of the paragraph, but the student does insert his or her own ideas. As students gain confidence as writers, they will not need such extensive support.

It is important to recognize that the graphic organizer is *not* the only scaffold needed. The key to success is practice, practice, and more practice before independent paragraph writing is attempted. Too many students who take the time to fill out a graphic organizer or make tremendous "story webs" never use this information in their writing. They don't understand how to classify the information from the graphic organizer and how to take their numerous ideas, glean the important ones, and then turn them into sentences. They don't have the skills necessary to organize the information from the organizer to make it useful or meaningful. In essence, when they are required to make a graphic organizer and then write a paragraph, they have to do double the work, as the two are rarely related to each other. They do not make the connection between the two without practice and the support of the teacher. Only through direct instruction, support in clarifying how to classify the information from the brainstorm list, and then support in converting those ideas to a graphic organizer and then sentence formation can students with ADHD truly become independent paragraph writers.

Editing and Final Draft

For children with ADHD, this tedious step is almost as difficult and frustrating as the actual writing process. Children with ADHD are not detail oriented and will probably not catch spelling or punctuation errors independently. Editing is best left to the teacher, an older peer, or a paraprofessional. One appropriate editing strategy according to Fink-Chorzempka and colleagues (2005) is to have students read their writing orally to another person to edit their own mistakes in word order and so forth. Requiring students to edit independently will only cause further frustration. Allowing them to write using a computer with spell check and grammar check will enable them to use those tools to edit their own work and should be encouraged. For younger children, direct teacher support will be needed.

The final draft step is equally as frustrating to a child with ADHD. Those who have struggled with getting the ideas into correct sentence form with appropriate word use, spelling, and conventions do not want to do it *again*!

Form 6.2   Paragraph Scaffold

_____ are interesting animals.

They eat _____.

They often live in _____.

They like to eat _____.

I think _____.

They have toiled through the entire multistep writing process, only to be required to copy "in their best handwriting" work that they have already done. Not too many students with ADHD will persist through this step without much complaining and consternation, especially since fine motor weaknesses are common for them. This step is easily avoided if the child is allowed to use a keyboarding device such as an Alpha Smart or a computer. Another option for younger students is to have a "secretary" retype the final draft for the student. Teachers also need to determine if there is a need for a perfect final draft for all writing assignments. Again, if the objective of the assignment is a written paragraph, should the handwriting matter? Does all work need to be in "published" form?

THE DREADED BOOK REPORT!

For parents of young school-age children with ADHD, there are few homework assignments that bring more dread than the book report. This is *not* due to the fact that students with ADHD cannot comprehend what they have read, it comes from the fact that they lack the skill to organize the story events in a sequential manner. This is where the scaffold of a good graphic organizer can help students get past the "too many details" stage. In this graphic organizer (see Form 6.3), the student starts with what happened at the beginning of the story, as Event 1, and what happened at the end of the story, as Event 5. Most students who have actually read the book will be able to do these two tasks. The next box that is filled in is Event 3; this is the middle of the story, or the part where the problem of the story becomes a real issue, or where things usually change for the worse. Most students can identify this as well. Now that the three main points of beginning, middle, and end are in place, the paper is unfolded to reveal the boxes for Event 2 and Event 4. These are the events that occurred between the beginning and the middle, Event 2, and what happened between the middle and the end, Event 4. This Event 4 is usually the climax of the story, with the end being the resolution. The student now has these five events to sequence either into a nice five-sentence summary or book report. Again, the graphic organizer has provided the structure to organize the sequence of the story events to support the students in writing a summary.

Although there are many wonderful book report ideas, a summary of some type is almost always required. Hopefully for most book reports, this would be the only written part that is required. If the teacher has assigned the book report for the purpose of checking on a student's understanding of the story, there are many other options to choose from rather than a written assignment. Students can make a film strip of the main characters, setting, and story events, or they can make a book jacket with this same information

Form 6.3   Graphic Organizer for Book Report

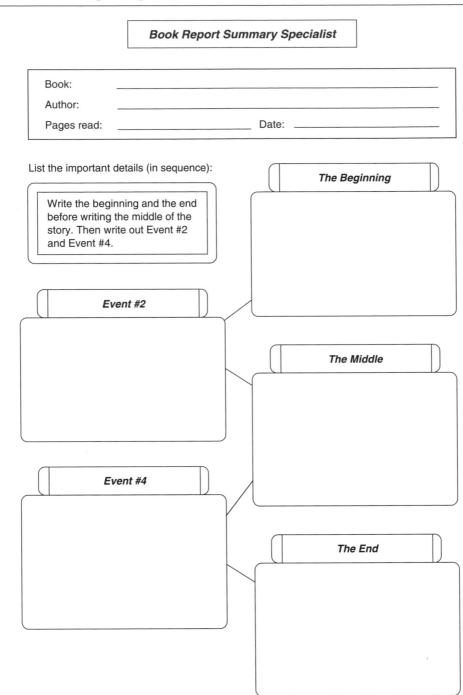

using pictures and drawings to convey these elements. The key again is to determine what is actually being assessed, and if writing is not the objective, students should have other options to share their knowledge.

THE EVEN MORE DREADED WRITTEN REPORT

There is only one more dreaded assignment to any child with ADHD than the book report, and that is the written report. Today, even first and second graders are being required to meet standards in these areas. The difficulty with this assignment is that it not only requires the multiple steps and organization necessary for writing, but also the ability to research a topic and take that information and convey it in students' "own words" into a written report format. The instructions to find only the important information and then incorporate into some kind of coherent, multipage, written document is like asking a child with ADHD to create the human body from a single cell. They feel overwhelmed and find that without the help of parents, they cannot figure out how to navigate through the process. In most instances, frustrated parents end up doing the assignment for them.

Tackling Research

What seems to be the most difficult aspect of this assignment is the research. Students do not understand exactly what this is. It is words written on index cards that you copy from a book or from the Internet. For students who do not typically have sustained attention or the ability to persist, this process is more than tedious, and they find it nearly impossible to complete successfully. The practice that has helped students be able to meet this monster head on is to first break the giant into doable parts. Students take the parts required, usually categorized sections, and with the support of a parent or teacher, break the tasks up into what needs to be done each day. If only one section is required each day, the child may actually feel capable of being able to accomplish that single specific task. Next, the illusive concept of "research" must be attacked. According to Patty Schetter (2004) in her work with students who suffer from anxiety disorders, she has found that linking research to something that students already routinely do helps to reduce the anxiety and stress that comes with it. Many young grade-school students are adept at using Google on the Internet to research ways to beat a video game or to find out the latest on their Neopet. Unfortunately, students do not see this process as research and do not make the connection that this is something that they already know how to do. Making this connection for them helps them see that research is doable and can be done without undue stress.

Once this connection is made, the teacher and student, or parent and student, should brainstorm questions that the student may have about the topic of the report. These questions can be written on cards or typed into the computer. This is the basis of their research . . . simply put, it is answering questions that you have about something. The student then can access materials that might provide the answers to those questions. The answers can be written on the index cards or simply written on paper in complete sentences or typed on some keyboarding device. Some of the most common report topics with research questions have been provided to elementary teachers in the book *Report Writing: Removing the Stress!* (DeRuvo & DeRuvo, 2000).

When the students have answered these questions in complete sentences, they will find that they usually have a simple report already written. These sentences may need to be rearranged to put information on specific topics in the same paragraph, but that can easily be done if the sentences are written on cards or on a computer or keyboarding device, such as an Alpha Smart. If the student has not used a computer, there is still the last step of writing the final draft. Again, with the fine motor issues that children with ADHD face, they should be allowed to type the report or have a parent, teacher, or another student play the role of the "secretary" and type the finished document from the rough draft. Again, this is not "cheating" as some may see it; it is simply leveling the playing field for a child who would spend more than a few nights copying something that he or she has already spent hours writing. Most children with ADHD would not persist through this process and would again taste failure, rather than success. When chunked into doable parts and given the scaffold of questions to guide research and the support of a secretary or a keyboarding device, students with ADHD can be successful even with this difficult assignment.

SUMMARY

Children with ADHD, like all other children, will develop writing skills if provided specific scaffolding and support to navigate the steps of the writing process. With the step-by-step support and modeling provided by effective teachers, students can learn to let their creativity shine, even through the written word. We hope these strategies will help them become successful writers and ultimately successful students.

What Teachers Should Know About Medication

7

David Rosenthal, MD

> A mother, after being confronted by a pharmacy assistant, reported feeling angry, embarrassed, and hurt. When she picked up her child's medication at the pharmacy, the assistant told her, "I wouldn't put my child on Ritalin, and you should think twice about giving your child Ritalin." The mother left feeling attacked and guilt ridden.

Medicating children for ADHD continues to be controversial, especially in light of the dramatic increase in the number of prescriptions being written for stimulant medications in the past few years across the United States. An outspoken physician and writer, Peter Breggin (1998), advocates stopping the current trend in medicating children for ADHD. He argues that not only is Ritalin uncalled for on many occasions, but that it can have serious side effects that are not brought to parents' attention. He writes that "the debate about Ritalin and ADHD has been lopsided" (Breggin, 1998). He suggests that teachers, much like parents, feel pressured to find shortcuts for dealing with the disruptive and fidgety child and that support groups and drug companies for both political and financial reasons are misleading them. The consequence is that more and more American children are now being medicated for ADHD.

The media regularly add to the controversy by producing headlines that are designed to attract attention and do not always accurately transmit scientific facts. For example: "Michigan ranks third in nation in prescribing Ritalin: Some say schools turn to medication to control students. Ritalin's routine use raises alarm over diagnosis, goals. Use of Ritalin in schools nearly out of control" (1998). However, according to a report by the American

Medical Association's Council of Scientific Affairs (1998), overprescription of drugs to treat the disorder is not widespread. Dr. Richard Nakamura (2002), acting director of the National Institute of Mental Health, in his testimony before the Committee on Government Reform, U.S. House of Representatives, stated that

> little evidence of overdiagnosis of ADHD or overprescription of stimulant medications has been verified in research. Indeed, fewer children (2% to 3% of school-aged children) are being treated for ADHD than suffer from it. Treatment rates are much lower for girls, minorities, and children receiving care through public service systems.

Parents and other caregivers may find themselves wondering how they can possibly decide whether to medicate their children when doctors themselves can't seem to agree. Teachers, like parents, will often express reservations about the issue of medicating children for ADHD.

This chapter is not intended to promote or to dispute the claims of others about the role of medication in the treatment of ADHD, but rather to educate teachers on the current medications used in the treatment of ADHD, the limitations of medication, and parental concerns that teachers should be aware of.

Professional disagreement and continuing dialogue is important and helpful to clinicians working with children who have ADHD. We support parents trying behavioral interventions and school accommodations before medication is administered to very young children. There is research suggesting that behavior modification should be started first and that medication should be considered when parent resources are limited for therapy and there is considerable room for improvement (Pelham & Fabiano, 2001; Pisterman et al., 1989). We concur and believe that the medical dictum "first, do no harm" should guide any ADHD intervention. Medication has been proven to be the most effective intervention in addressing core ADHD symptoms; however, with very young children, we feel that other clinically and educationally recognized interventions should be attempted first.

When medication is decided on, it can play an important role in the treatment of ADHD. Despite concerns about stigma and medication side effects, a decision *not* to treat ADHD with medication may have significant negative consequences for a child both in terms of school performance as well as with the multiple social and secondary psychological problems that can occur if impulsivity and socially inappropriate behaviors are left unchecked. For example, studies show that untreated ADHD children experience greater peer rejection, have higher injury rates, and experience higher rates of substance abuse and antisocial behavior. Their families experience high rates of marital discord, parental frustration, and divorce (Bloomquist, 1996). Parents and other caregivers do not have an easy choice in deciding whether to have their child take medication. It is important to respect the difficulty of this decision and keep in mind that families are considering all benefits, risks, and side effects involved.

This chapter overviews the importance of ongoing communication, with signed permission, between the teacher and the child's doctor once a child is started on medication. A young child can spend four to six hours in school, and a teacher's feedback on the child's behaviors while on medication is very important in helping the doctor measure the effectiveness of medication and assess the need for changes in dosage. The chapter also looks at some common side effects from ADHD medications. It is important that teachers are aware of possible side effects they may recognize in the classroom. The information provided in this chapter follows a question-and-answer format that we hope is easy to follow.

What medications are most commonly used to treat ADHD?

While there are a number of potentially useful medications for treating ADHD, the vast majority of children will be tried first on a stimulant medication, and most of the discussion in this chapter will be focused on treatment with stimulants. Stimulant medications are typically first choices primarily because this class of medication has been available for many years and stimulants have a long, relatively safe track record when used appropriately. There are few potentially serious side effects associated with these medicines, and they are relatively easy to administer and are available in a wide variety of brand names and "delivery systems." Stimulants have consistently been demonstrated to improve attention, hyperactivity, and impulsivity significantly better than placebos in numerous studies (well over 300 studies involving stimulant usage in children with ADHD have been published). While there are numerous stimulants currently on the market in the United States, most can be subcategorized into either the "methylphenidate-based" stimulant products (e.g., Ritalin, Concerta, Metadate, Focalin, Daytrana) or the "methamphetamine-based" stimulant products (e.g., Dexedrine, Adderall). Within each stimulant class, products differ primarily in how rapidly they take effect and in how long they continue to exert their behavioral and cognitive effects (see Table 7.1).

Generally, about 75% of all children with ADHD will respond well to a methylphenidate stimulant, and for those who don't seem to get an optimal response or who don't seem to tolerate methylphenidate products, about 75% of these children will then respond well to a methamphetamine product. The

Table 7.1   Medication Table

Stimulant Generic Name	Stimulant Trade Name	Typical Dosage Range in mg/dose	Onset of Behavioral Effect in Minutes	Approximate Duration of Action in Hours
Methylphenidate	Ritalin	5–20	20–30	3–4
Methylphenidate (sustained release)	Ritalin SR	10–40	45–60	6–8
Methylphenidate (extended release)	Metadate ER	10–40	45–60	6–8
Methylphenidate (immediate + extended release)	Metadate CD	10–40	20–30	6–8
Methylphenidate (long acting)	Ritalin LA	10–40	20–30	6–8
Methylphenidate (extended release)	Concerta	18–72	20–30	11–12
Methylphenidate adhesive patch	Daytrana	10–30	60–120	10–12
Dexmethylphenidate	Focalin	2.5–10	20–30	3–4
Dexmethylphenidate (extended release)	Focalin XR	5–20	20–30	6–8
Dextroamphetamine	Dexedrine	2.5–10	20–30	3–4
Dextroamphetamine (sustained release)	Dexedrine Spansules	5–20	45–60	6–8
Mixed amphetamine salts	Adderall	5–20	20–30	5–6
Mixed amphetamine salts	Adderall XR	10–40	20–30	10–12
Pemoline	Cylert	37.5–112.5	45–60	6–12

SOURCE: David Rosenthal, MD.

converse is also true if a methamphetamine product is the first medication tried (although in my personal clinical experience with many thousands of patients with ADHD, methylphenidate products tend to be slightly less potent or "robust" than methamphetamine products due to a difference in the way they work in the brain, but methylphenidate products are better tolerated by a larger proportion of patients).

A review of Table 7.1 reveals that most stimulants begin to take effect within the first hour of administration. There are several older, "short-acting" stimulant preparations that actively exert their effects for three to four hours. In the past several years, a great deal of research has been done to develop progressively longer-acting stimulant medications to effectively treat symptoms continuously throughout the entire school day. Medications such as Concerta, Adderall XR, and now Daytrana (a methylphenidate patch designed to be placed on the child's hip in the morning and removed daily after nine hours) can provide symptom relief for 10 to 12 hours daily and give children the ability to maintain their concentration and attention on late afternoon or early evening projects or homework, with the convenience and improvement in medication compliance offered by once daily medication.

Although the methylphenidate and methamphetamine products have traditionally been and continue to be prescribed as the "first line" treatment of ADHD in children, several other medications can be used, particularly when stimulants are not tolerated or are not completely effective by themselves.

Atomoxetine (Strattera) was approved by the FDA in November, 2002 for the treatment of ADHD in children, adolescents, and adults. Strattera is a nonstimulant medication with stimulant-like properties. It is often used in children who fail to tolerate or fail to respond to traditional stimulants. At low doses, which are less stimulating but often less effective for treating core ADHD symptoms than higher doses, Strattera may have a calming effect and often helps children who have high levels of anxiety along with their ADHD. For children who benefit from but don't tolerate sufficient doses of stimulants to get a full response, adding low-dose Strattera to the stimulant is a strategy employed by an increasing number of physicians. Parents and teachers need to be aware that unlike the stimulants, which deliver an immediate response once the "optimal" dose is found, Strattera may need to be given daily for up to two months in children before its effectiveness can be fully ascertained, and most doctors feel that response rates overall to Strattera tend to be much lower than response rates to stimulants.

Bupropion (Wellbutrin) is an antidepressant with stimulant properties that is frequently used in adolescents, and less frequently used in children, as there are very limited studies assessing Wellbutrin in the pediatric population. It is most typically used by doctors to treat ADHD when depression is also present, but it has been shown to have some efficacy in the treatment of nondepressed children with ADHD (Conners et al., 1996). Response rates to Wellbutrin tend to be low compared with response rates to stimulants, but stimulants in low doses can be safely combined with conservative doses of Wellbutrin if needed.

The "alpha-agonists" *clonidine (Catapress)* and *guanfacine (Tenex)* are nonstimulants (traditionally used as blood pressure medications at high doses) and are most commonly used in combination with stimulants to control hyperactivity, impulsivity, aggression, insomnia, tics, and oppositional-defiant symptoms when these problems are associated with ADHD (Arnsten, Steere, & Hunt, 1996; Chappell et al., 1995; Hunt, Arnsten, & Asbell, 1995; Scahill et al., 2001). They can be sedating but very helpful.

The tricyclic antidepressants (e.g., *imipramine, desipramine, nortriptyline*) are an older class of nonstimulant medications that have been shown to be effective for ADHD in children, but they have been less commonly used in the past few years, since they tend to be less effective than stimulants and often have annoying side effects (like sedation, dry mouth, constipation, and, rarely, cardiac side effects) that limit their use. They are most commonly used in those unusual circumstances in which stimulants are having a tendency to cause or exacerbate underlying motor tics or when enuresis (urinary incontinence) is a problem along with a child's ADHD symptoms.

Until recently, if a low-dose stimulant was effective at treating symptoms of inattention only, then it had been the preferred practice to simply raise the dosage higher and higher in a sometimes futile attempt to effectively target impulsivity and hyperactivity. This approach does work for some children, but in many cases, this just leads to the emergence of more side effects from the medicine with little further improvement in symptoms. Despite concerns about using more than one medication at a time, many practitioners, parents, and teachers have found that using two medications together at low doses may yield a dramatically greater response and treat more of the child's symptoms with fewer associated side effects than does using a high-dose stimulant alone.

There are many additional adjunctive medications currently available to treat symptoms or disorders that coexist with ADHD.

What changes can I expect to see with my students on stimulants?

While stimulants appear to have some potential to help with the full spectrum of ADHD symptoms, their greatest strength tends to lie with their ability to improve one's capacity to maintain focus and to stay on task. Studies have also noted overall improvement with stimulants in social situations, in that the medication tends to reduce the intensity and improve the quality of peer interactions. Impulse control, fine motor coordination, restlessness, reaction time, and even short-term memory have been shown to improve as well. Aggressive behavior is often reduced with stimulants, but frequently, the addition of secondary medications and additional behavior management techniques are necessary to control problematic aggressive behavior or severe emotional outbursts.

Do stimulants cure ADHD? How do these medicines work?

Unfortunately, no known medication actually cures ADHD. Medicines may, however, help to control many of the symptoms and behaviors associated with ADHD. Stimulant medications fundamentally work by increasing levels of the neurotransmitters norepinephrine and dopamine in areas of the brain that are relatively underactive in those with ADHD (thereby "stimulating" these areas). Underactive structures that are involved in moderating motor activity and distractibility become more "aroused" (see Chapter 1 under "What Causes ADHD?" for a more detailed discussion).

How long does a child with ADHD need to be on medication before it works?

As noted earlier, most stimulants exert their effects within the first hour of administration and are in the system for the next 3 to 12 hours, depending on the specific stimulant given. Consequently, on a given dosage, one should theoretically know if the medicine is effective shortly after the first dose. These medicines don't generally need repeated administration of a specific dose for one to know if they are going to be helpful. In reality, however, it isn't always easy to assess effectiveness after one dose, and it may take a few days to know for certain just how helpful a particular dose of the medicine is. Perhaps the most common reason for uncertainty is that there are any number of daily events or stresses in a child's life that potentially influence behavior. If, for example, a child in your classroom is upset because he has just been grounded by his parents for failing to do his household chores for the past six days in a row, then it is unlikely that he will suddenly be cooperative and focused on his schoolwork the day he gets his first dose of Ritalin. In other words, a pattern of responsiveness or failure to respond to a particular dose of a new medication is necessary to rule out the possibility that the child just had an unusually good or bad day when assessing medication effectiveness. If uncertain, it's important to communicate with the parent or doctor about any questions you may have regarding the child's behavior.

How will I know if my student is overmedicated?

Enough medicine is when you see significant improvement in a child's ADHD symptoms without significant side effects (Breggin, 1998). The most common sign indicating that too much medicine is being given is either:

a. The child looks "wired." He or she looks more hyperactive, seems jittery or shaky, and is more anxious and uncomfortable. All the ADHD symptoms seem worse.

b. He or she looks lethargic or looks as though he or she is withdrawn and without any of the usual spunk. If a child looks lethargic, you should communicate this observation to the parent and doctor.

If the medicine works, does that confirm that the diagnosis of ADHD is correct?

Not necessarily. Stimulants, including caffeine, tend to improve attention in most people at some dosage. For example, if 5 or 10 milligrams of Ritalin were given to 100 children or adults, we would likely note measurable improvement in attention and in freedom from distractibility in the majority of these individuals. Those few who don't respond are usually either (a) individuals who are unusually sensitive to annoying or adverse side effects to stimulants, or (b) those who have coexisting problems with their ADHD such as severe anxiety, depression, or bipolar disorder. The crucial point here, however, is that in those individuals identified as having the greatest problem with attention, that is, those with ADHD, we would likely see very dramatic pre- versus poststimulant differences in these individuals' ability to attend to a particular task. Those individuals with no notable problem focusing in the first place, however, would likely only see minor improvements in their ability to focus after taking the low-dose Ritalin. In summary, then, while a positive response to stimulants won't diagnose ADHD, in most cases, those who do have ADHD will respond significantly.

What are the possible side effects of stimulants that my student might experience?

Although the extreme abuse of stimulants in adults has been known to cause central nervous system damage, vascular damage, and hypertension, virtually none of these problems are known to occur with the standard dosages used to treat ADHD symptoms. The vast majority of healthy children prescribed routine doses of stimulants have either no significant side effects or mild, tolerable side effects. Most side effects are dose related, so that the higher the dose used, the greater the likelihood that some annoying side effect will emerge. At routine doses, it is extraordinarily rare to see any medically dangerous side effects in a healthy child. Nonetheless, we recommend that all children being evaluated for stimulant treatment have a thorough physical examination to look for any underlying medical conditions that might increase the child's risk of having problems with the medication. Once a stimulant is started, growth, weight, and blood pressure should be monitored with routine visits to the medical doctor.

Common Side Effects From Stimulants

Appetite Suppression. The most common side effect in children that I encounter from stimulants is appetite suppression. In most cases, this side effect is easily managed by simply administering the stimulant with or following meals. Sometimes, switching a child to an alternate stimulant will cause less appetite suppression. Another alternative is to do nothing and to see if the appetite suppression, if mild, will simply resolve in the next few weeks on its own with continued use of the stimulant, as frequently is the case. If all else fails, doctors can add a medicine such as an antihistamine to stimulate appetite, but this is almost never necessary. Feeding children high-calorie, healthy foods before the stimulant takes effect and after the stimulant wears off is usually sufficient.

Insomnia. Another common but easily managed side effect is insomnia. As most of us who use caffeine know, taking a stimulant too close to bedtime can cause insomnia. Simply adjusting the timing of the dosing so that the stimulant is out of the system by bedtime will solve the problem in most cases. For kids whose ADHD itself is the primary reason they have trouble falling asleep, sometimes an evening dose of a stimulant actually allows for improvement in the insomnia by decreasing the hyperactive behavior and the difficulty "gearing down" for bed that is so often seen in these children. If all else fails, low doses of other medications such as Benadryl (diphenhydramine), or Catapress (clonidine), given at bedtime, can be used to help a child get to sleep whether the stimulant is contributing to the problem or not. There are also a wide variety of over-the-counter herbal teas and preparations that can help with this problem.

Mild Headaches or Stomach Upset. Mild headaches or stomach upset are occasionally noted with a particular stimulant. Usually these two side effects rapidly resolve on their own with continued use of the stimulant but, if not, a dosage decrease or a change in the kind of stimulant used, or even a change in the drug manufacturer (if generic stimulants are prescribed) will most often help.

Rebound Effect. The rebound effect is another common but generally manageable phenomenon that can occur when stimulant medication rapidly wears off. It is characterized by irritability and an exacerbation of those baseline ADHD symptoms that are noted without medication, such as impulsivity and hyperactivity. Sometimes the child's mood is depressed but, in any event, it is an unpleasant experience if your student has this each time the stimulant wears off. Fortunately, these symptoms, when present, will tend to only last for 30 to 60 minutes followed by a return to the child's baseline.

With the widespread use of longer acting stimulants, rebound effect is much less common than it used to be when only shorter acting stimulants were available. The long-acting preparations tend to leave the system more slowly and hence have a lower likelihood of causing this problem. One can also try overlapping dosages by always giving the second stimulant dose (when using a short-acting stimulant) at least 20 to 30 minutes before the rebound effect occurs from the first dose wearing off. Since rebound effects are dose related, if the second stimulant dosage is lower than the first dose, the risk of rebound when the second dose wears off will be reduced.

Common Side Effects With Strattera

The most common side effects noted with Strattera (atomoxetine) are abdominal discomfort, nausea, decreased appetite, irritability, and drowsiness. Most of these side effects are transient and manageable if the child's dosage is increased very slowly over several weeks.

What information from teachers is helpful to doctors?

Good communication between the teacher and the doctor is extremely valuable, particularly when starting or adjusting medications. Unfortunately, many physicians have practices that severely limit their ability to communicate on the phone, so teachers are often left feeling that their input is not valued. On the contrary, a teacher has the unique experience of being able to observe large numbers of children of a particular age group, so he or she may be the first observer to notice when a particular child is functioning outside the norm. This knowledge and information is critical for the physician in his or her assessment of the child. Ongoing observations by the teacher are also essential when deciding whether a medication is being administered at the optimal dosage, especially if a shorter acting stimulant is being used for school only, in which case the teacher may be the only adult who has direct knowledge of the response to the medication or of any problematic side effects such as excessive sedation or agitation. Once the parent signs the appropriate consent form, your observations can be communicated by fax, e-mail, or phone to the physician's ancillary staff (physician assistant, nurse, or nurse practitioner) if the doctor is unavailable.

Are stimulants addictive?

Although prescription stimulants like Ritalin, Dexedrine, and Adderall all carry strong warnings regarding their "addictive potential," in practice, actual drug addiction (or "drug dependence," as is now the preferred and more precise term) is quite rare when these medications are used as prescribed. Two of the most important components of drug dependence are (a) tolerance and (b) withdrawal. *Tolerance* refers to either a need to take progressively higher doses of a medication to achieve the desired effect, or it refers to a diminished effect with continued use of the same amount of the substance. As most of us are aware, drugs such as nicotine, alcohol, Valium, and even the stimulant caffeine are associated with the development of significant tolerance. Most readers of this book who drink several cups of coffee daily can readily attest to this phenomenon from their personal experience. These same drugs also have significant withdrawal syndromes associated with their abrupt discontinuation. Again, many of us who have tried abruptly withholding our own coffee for a few days after drinking several cups daily are well aware of the severe fatigue and withdrawal headaches we often experience.

With respect to the issue of tolerance, prescription stimulants prescribed for ADHD in standard dosages rarely result in the development of tolerance (since caffeine is the notable exception among the stimulants, it is not a particularly good drug for treating ADHD). If tolerance does develop, the medication can be discontinued for several days and then restarted at the previous dosage or changed to a different stimulant as there is rarely any significant cross-tolerance from one stimulant to the next. Thus, the stimulants do not need to be used on a daily basis to be effective and can be discontinued abruptly at any time if desired without any adverse medical consequences. Obviously, the underlying ADHD symptoms will rapidly return with medication discontinuation, as stimulants will not cure ADHD but will merely treat symptoms of ADHD while the medication is in the bloodstream.

Can stimulants lead to problems with abuse of other drugs?

Children with untreated ADHD are already at higher than average risk for substance abuse for several possible reasons. Poor impulse control, low self-esteem, defiant behavior, and impairment in social skills are all commonly seen in children with ADHD, and any of these factors would tend to increase one's eventual risk of experimenting with or abusing illicit drugs as a teenager or adult.

Consequently, there would be justifiable concern if such risk were to somehow be further increased by the treatment of ADHD with powerful stimulant drugs. Many teachers and parents worry that giving a child a pill might give them the message that pills are an easy way to solve life's problems, or that the "addictiveness" of stimulants might multiply the risk of abusing other drugs.

Current studies on this issue actually suggest that stimulant use for treatment of ADHD does *not* lead to later abuse of other drugs. There is, in fact, evidence to suggest that aggressive treatment of ADHD may actually *decrease* the likelihood of abusing other drugs, perhaps because aggressive treatment over time may directly or indirectly reduce many of the factors noted previously, which put children with ADHD at risk in the first place.

This is not to say that the use of stimulants is risk free. Treatment with stimulants needs to be considered only with great caution, for instance, in teens that are already identified to be abusing other drugs. When substance abuse is an issue but ADHD needs to be treated, Strattera, Provigil, Wellbutrin, and Concerta (methylphenidate in a delivery system with low abuse potential) are all reasonable options and alternatives to the traditional stimulants. With respect to the relevant concern that giving a pill to a child sends a negative message, it is always important to teach children the difference between taking a pill to treat a legitimate medical problem versus the indiscriminate use and abuse of mood-altering drugs to either get high or to escape reality.

Are there particular kids who would be expected to do poorly on stimulants?

While there are few absolute contraindications to the use of stimulants, there are certain groups for whom stimulants are generally either not recommended or for whom they should be used with greater caution. The first of these would include those with psychotic disorders such as schizophrenia, in whom stimulants have the potential to exacerbate psychotic symptoms such as paranoia or auditory hallucinations. The routine use of stimulants would not normally be expected to cause any of these symptoms in children with a diagnosis of ADHD alone, but might do so in psychotic children with schizophrenia or bipolar disorder, if their inattentiveness is mistaken for ADHD.

Similarly, any child with severe anxiety would be at risk for an exacerbation of his or her anxiety with the use of a stimulant medication. This group would include either those children who seem biologically predisposed to having high levels of anxiety or those children who are highly anxious or worried due to situational circumstances. An example might be the child who lives in a chaotic family environment or one who has been traumatized emotionally by significant abuse or neglect.

In the case of the anxious child with ADHD, the stimulant has the potential to help with the ADHD, but the stimulant will also have the potential to worsen ADHD symptoms by exacerbating the anxiety. Likewise for depressed children with underlying ADHD, stimulants may at times appear mildly helpful, but if the depressive disorder is significant, then the child's ADHD symptoms will not likely improve to any meaningful degree until the depression is adequately treated.

Other situations in which stimulants are not consistently helpful might include their use in the treatment of children who appear to have ADHD-like symptoms associated with intrauterine drug exposure, traumatic brain injuries, or pervasive developmental disorders such as autism. These are not hard and fast rules, as some children in these groups may respond positively to stimulants, but children in these categories appear to be at higher than average risk for a worsening of their behavioral problems with the use of stimulants.

Stimulants also are not likely to directly improve learning disabilities or oppositional-defiant disorders, but they may help if ADHD is clearly present underlying or alongside these problems. The use of stimulants in children with substance abuse problems is another category in which there is a relative contraindication as was discussed earlier.

Are there children who need to be on medication only at school?

While there is perhaps no correct answer to this question, my own philosophy is to recommend stimulant medication every day for those children with ADHD whose impulsivity or hyperactivity leads to emotional outbursts or behavioral problems that improve whenever the stimulant is taken. In these children, withholding medication on weekends doesn't make sense if the inevitable outcome is eruption into chaos. Increasingly, I am recommending medication daily for the majority of children with ADHD that I treat (even in those without serious behavior problems) because so many of them have multiple deficits that tend to improve with medication, and because there are so few problems associated with taking the medication daily (as noted previously, tolerance, appetite suppression, and insomnia from the medication are rarely a significant problem).

On the other hand, there are some children with ADHD who have no unusual social or behavioral problems and are primarily taking the stimulant to improve attention in the classroom or to complete homework after school. Therefore, unless there is some unusual activity to complete on a weekend or holiday that requires a great deal of attention, it is not mandatory for these children to take their stimulants on weekends or holidays, especially since there is typically no identified set of symptoms associated with abrupt discontinuation of stimulants, that is, a withdrawal syndrome.

Are there problems with adverse drug interactions if a child is on a stimulant?

There are very few problematic drug interactions with stimulants, but there may be times, as a teacher, that you observe a child who appears to vary in his or her response to a stable dose of medication on different days without any apparent environmental or "untreated mood component" to his or her ADHD to explain the problem.

One possible, and infrequently recognized, cause might be the combination of the stimulant at breakfast with what are known as *organic acids* such as ascorbic acid (vitamin C) or citric acid (in orange or cranberry juice). Other possible culprits include oral suspension antibiotics, Pop Tarts, Power Bars, granola bars, and Gatorade. All of these substances, which can create an acidic stomach environment, can interfere with proper absorption of the medication and are best avoided for at least 30 to 45 minutes before or after taking the medication if a consistent response to a particular dose of a stimulant is desired. The methylphenidate-based, long-acting medications Concerta (taken orally) and Daytrana (the methylphenidate patch) appear to be largely unaffected by these issues due to their unique delivery systems (Auiler, Liu, Lynch, & Gelotte, 2002). Once the medication begins to take effect, these acidic substances are no longer a problem. Grapefruit juice, however, presents its own unique problem in that it contains enzymes which may cause dramatic *increases* in absorption of a variety of medications. Consequently, I recommend avoiding grapefruit juice entirely in anyone taking medication unless a pharmacist is able to verify that there is no interaction with the specific medication that the child is taking.

It is important that you share with the parent any behaviors that seem unusual or raise questions in your mind. The parent should be encouraged to share your thoughts with the child's doctor.

I've heard that kids can become psychotic on stimulants. Is it true?

Stimulants used appropriately in the absence of any disorder associated with psychotic symptoms (e.g., schizophrenia or bipolar disorder) will not normally cause psychotic symptoms. In rare cases, it may be possible to induce temporary psychotic symptoms in susceptible individuals by administering stimulants far in excess of their recommended dosages. Prolonged abuse of stimulants at many times their recommended dosage may eventually lead to a "schizophrenic-like" presentation but this is simply not an issue with judicious use of prescription stimulants.

Can stimulants be used by children younger than age five?

Yes, but with several caveats. Recent estimates suggest that only 0.3% of children younger than age six are being treated with stimulant medications and that the rate of use in the preschool-age group did not increase in the five-year period studied (Zuvekas, Vitiello, & Norquist, 2006). There are several reasons for caution. First, stimulant use is not well studied in children this young, and there are theoretical concerns about exposing very young children to stimulants (especially children younger than four years of age) when so little is known about how these medications may affect very early brain development, although no unique medical problems have been identified in children younger than age five that would absolutely contraindicate stimulant usage. Perhaps an equally important reason to withhold prescribing in children this young is that it is difficult to be certain in this age group whether the ADHD diagnosis is accurate, even though the majority of children who later turn out to actually have diagnosable ADHD in grade school do historically manifest symptoms of ADHD prior to first grade. In such young children, it can be difficult to fully evaluate other problems that can mimic ADHD, such as developmental disabilities or simple immaturity. In addition, most of the psychological tests used in an educational setting to assess for the presence of learning disabilities are simply not available for use in such young children (Firestone, Musten, Pisterman, Mercer, & Bennett, 1998; Minde, 1998; Rappley et al., 1999; Short, Manos, Findling, & Schubel, 2004; Zito et al., 2000).

Another complicating variable is that commercially available doses of many stimulants may be too potent for such small children, and it can be difficult to divide some stimulant preparations into small enough fractions of a pill to be practical (this is becoming less of a problem over time with so many different stimulant products now available). Longer acting stimulant preparations are preferred in young children, since this population tends to metabolize the short-acting stimulant preparations very rapidly, necessitating frequent dosing throughout the day (which is often impractical). Frequent dosing of short-acting stimulants can lead to potentially significant rebound effects. Other problematic side effects to stimulants in this population are sadness, irritability, insomnia, loss of appetite, and clinginess. Under these circumstances the child, parent, and teacher may feel like the child is on a mood roller coaster. Consequently, it is advisable to wait until grade school, if possible, before placing a child on medication, although, in severe cases, waiting may not always be practical, especially if other behavioral interventions are not effective.

My student used to do well on Ritalin, but now it doesn't seem to work. What is going on?

If the issue is an on again–off again response to stimulants in which the medicine seems to work well at times and then not to work at all, then the possibility of an underlying mood disorder is suggested. Mood disorders usually interfere with one's ability to attend and to concentrate, so that one's ADHD symptoms will appear to be at their worst when mood symptoms are prominent. If ADHD symptoms tend to disappear completely when one's mood is normal while other home and school variables are unchanged, then the actual diagnosis of ADHD becomes doubtful. If ADHD symptoms are merely a bit less pronounced than usual when one's mood is stable, then ADHD *and* a mood disorder are likely to both be present.

If the issue is not an on again–off again problem but rather is simply that the medication no longer is as helpful as it used to be, then a slight dose increase may be indicated. It is possible that due to the child's growth, the medication is simply no longer effective at its current dosage. Another possibility is that some tolerance to the medication has developed over time. If tolerance seems to be the issue, it is worth asking the parent to speak with the doctor about a "drug holiday" to assess for this possibility. Unfortunately, temporary discontinuation of the medication may not always be practical if the child's behavior is unmanageable without the medication, in which case it may be necessary to switch to a different class of medication.

Are there any good natural remedies available for treating ADHD?

The term *natural remedies* generally refers to those substances used for medicinal purposes that are found in relatively unaltered states in the environment—as opposed to the *unnatural* pharmaceutical drugs which are synthesized in laboratories. Natural remedies are popularly thought of as safe, and synthetic, unnatural drugs are often considered by the lay public to be potentially hazardous. The problem with what seems to be a simple distinction, however, is that natural remedies are not always safe or adequately tested, and many are processed in unnatural ways before they reach the consumer. Furthermore, many pharmaceutical drugs are actually derived from natural sources, and some that are entirely synthetic may be quite safe or may be chemically indistinguishable from similar substances of natural origin. In other words, the boundaries between natural and unnatural remedies are fuzzy at best.

Nonetheless, using the previous definition, there may be some useful natural remedies available for treating conditions that mimic ADHD or conditions that may coexist with ADHD such as depressive or anxiety disorders. However, in my own practice I have yet to see any clear and significant treatment responses to herbal medicines, homeopathic treatments, or vitamin therapies for the treatment of the core symptoms of ADHD. Many dramatic claims have been touted for the use of remedies such as blue-green algae or other potent antioxidant preparations from pine bark or grapeseed extract, but thus far in my experience, the transient mild benefits noted by some parents seem to have ultimately amounted to little more than brief placebo responses.

Having said this, there may be a place for some use of certain supplements in small, select subgroups of children with ADHD. For example, ADHD has been found to be associated with a deficiency of essential fatty acids in some children (Colquhoun & Bunday, 1981), and that supplementing the diet with essential fatty acids (usually given in the form of fish oil) in these children may reduce ADHD symptoms (Burgess, 1998). While studies in this area are very promising, it should be emphasized that ADHD symptoms did not disappear entirely with fish oil alone and that the positive results were seen primarily in children who manifested clinical signs consistent with a deficiency of essential fatty acids, such as frequent urination, excessive thirst, dry skin, and dry hair (Mitchell, Aman, Turbott, & Manku, 1987). Other studies have suggested, for example, associations between ADHD and deficiencies of iron or zinc. Again, such deficiencies apply to very small percentages of children with ADHD symptoms and have little relevance to the vast majority of children, for whom genetic factors play the most important etiologic role in their ADHD. In response to observations that some children show hyperactive behavior associated with certain foods, especially sugar, food dyes, chocolate, and other additives, various "elimination" diets have been tried. The best known of these is the Feingold diet. Several double-blind, placebo-controlled studies have failed to support dietary effects of food additives or sugar on behavior, except, once again, possibly in a very small percentage of children (Egger, Stella, & McEwen, 1992; Wolraich, Wilson, & White, 1995).

The temptation to find a natural approach to treatment can be very strong. Most of us would like to use approaches to treatment that offer the greatest benefit with the fewest risks, but unfortunately, *natural* or *herbal* does not always mean *safer*. In addition, many parents feel that they can somehow avoid the stigma associated with either the ADHD diagnosis or with the use of stimulants by using alternative therapies instead.

Unfortunately, even if these approaches do not end up being toxic, they may have adverse consequences for a child if they significantly delay the usage of more thoroughly researched medications in which potential risks versus benefits are better known.

There is at least one important reason why natural treatments are often less well studied than are more traditional medications. Since natural remedies are by definition found in nature, these substances cannot, generally speaking, be easily patented by companies wishing to package and promote their use. The patent system was designed to give a person or company exclusive rights to research, to develop, and to market a product for a predetermined period of time. Once a patent is obtained, a company no longer needs to worry (for several years) that their own research and development dollars will allow a competing second or third company to borrow and profit from that research by marketing the same product with minimal investment. Therefore, without the ability to patent an herbal remedy, there traditionally has been little incentive for private companies to spend money on research. However, due to dramatic recent increases in the general public's interest in herbal remedies in the United States, there is increasing movement by both private enterprise and the government to fund research in this area.

Despite my not having personally seen any truly effective alternative medicines for ADHD thus far, this does not mean that I am entirely excluding the possibility that safe and effective alternative approaches will eventually be discovered.

One of my students is on Prozac. Is this commonly used in young children with ADHD?

Prozac (fluoxetine) is in a class of medications known as the "SSRIs" (selective serotonin re-uptake inhibitors). Other medications in this class are Zoloft (sertraline), Paxil (paroxetine), Luvox (fluvoxamine), Celexa (citalopram), and Lexapro (escitalopram). All are similar in their mechanism of action in the brain, yet all are slightly different from each other, and none will directly target the core symptoms of ADHD. Despite that fact, they are frequently used in children with ADHD when significant symptoms or signs of anxiety, depression, or obsessive-compulsiveness are present. The medications in this class can be extremely helpful for improving hyper-reactivity (as opposed to hyperactivity), in that when they are effective they tend to significantly improve a person's ability to take things in stride so that the person is less likely to become easily overwhelmed. This class of medication should be used cautiously, however, if bipolar disorder is suspected in the child, as the use of antidepressants without first using mood stabilizers could exacerbate manic symptoms or mood cycling in these cases. These medications need to be taken daily for maximum effectiveness, and missing doses can result in severe withdrawal agitation and dizziness in some cases.

Do medications help learning disabilities?

There really are no medications at this point in time that are known to directly improve learning disabilities (also known as developmental disorders). Nonetheless, if ADHD symptoms or other medication-responsive problems are present along with the learning disability, then at least the medication can effectively be used to target these areas. Once these associated treatable problems are better, the impairment from the disability itself can be more clearly seen and may appear to be less severe than originally thought.

One of my students is very defiant and oppositional. Will medications help with this?

Not directly in most cases. Oppositional defiant disorder (ODD) frequently is seen along with ADHD, especially in cases in which the ADHD goes untreated for several years. Kids with this problem are often irritable and angry and tend to lose their tempers often. They regularly argue with their parents and teachers and tend to blame someone else whenever they get into trouble. They actively defy rules and, in more severe cases, may eventually end up in trouble with the law.

Occasionally, these symptoms are part of an underlying depressive disorder, in which case the use of antidepressant medications will likely reduce the severity of these symptoms. More commonly, however, the ODD is not found to be associated with a depressive disorder, in which case, the appropriate treatment is to address the ADHD with medication and to learn as many of the other behavioral management strategies that you can from other sections in this book. Frequently, some direct improvement of ODD symptoms results from stimulant treatment alone. Often, improvement will come over time from the combination of stimulant treatment, appropriate behavioral management, and gradual improvement in self-esteem. Despite the absence of any universally acceptable medication for this problem, in desperation, many parents and psychiatrists will try medications such as antidepressants, alpha-agonists (Catapress or Tenex), neuroleptic medications (e.g., Abilify, Zyprexa, Seroquel, Risperdal), or anticonvulsants and mood stabilizers (e.g., Depakote, Lithium, Trileptal), in their attempt to mitigate the often-associated symptoms of impulsivity or aggression. At times, these other medications can be quite helpful.

SUMMARY

The decision a parent makes to medicate his or her child can be a difficult one. It's therefore important for teachers not only to show sympathy and understanding for the parent's anxiety and concerns about medicating his or her child for ADHD, but also to understand the benefits and limitations of medication in the treatment of ADHD. This chapter's intent was to inform you about the usefulness as well as the limitations of using medication and has tried to answer some of the most common questions that parents and teachers have about the actual use of specific medications for ADHD.

I discussed the various medications used to treat ADHD. I reviewed the most common side effects and complications associated with the use of stimulant medications and discussed the various options for managing problems that might arise in treatment.

Communicating Effectively With Parents

8

G ood communication with parents or primary caregivers of children
with ADHD is critical. No one person is more invested in or
knowledgeable about their child's life than they are. Sometimes it may not
be easy for us to tap into what parents and families know, but it is our
professional responsibility to mine the resources at our disposal. While some
parents require a good measure of "digging," we must remember that their
knowledge runs deep.

Teachers of very young children are generally the first people outside of
the family who will be seeing the child on a daily basis. A teacher often will be
the first outside caretaker who brings to the parent's attention the child's
behavioral challenges. Consequently, how teachers communicate concerns is
very important if they want to be successful in meeting the educational and
emotional needs of the child.

PARENTS: THE MOST IMPORTANT RESOURCE

For a number of reasons, parents are your most important resource and
partner in the education of their child.

Authors' Note: We recognize that children are raised by diverse groups of people who
go by diverse labels—parents, relatives, caregivers, guardians, and so forth. For
simplicity, we will use the word *parents* primarily throughout this chapter, intending
for it to encompass the variety of people who do the important work of parenting.

Parents Can Help You Better Understand Their Child's Learning Style

By the time a child enters preschool or kindergarten, the parents have spent many hours observing their child learn. They often can tell you what seems to work and not work when their child is introduced to new materials or activities. They know whether their child catches on easily or needs additional support to learn new materials. You can often learn by talking with the parent whether the child learns best verbally (auditorily), visually, or tactile-kinesthetically. As a verbal (auditory) learner, for example, the child is more likely to learn by listening, and a visual learner will learn by seeing. A tactile-kinesthetic learner will learn by touching and through movement.

Parents Can Help You Better Understand the Child's Temperament

The parents can tell you whether their child is an "easy child" who is generally positive and adapts easily to changes; a "slow to warm up" or shy child who typically withdraws in novel situations, displays negative mood at times, and is slow to adapt; and last, a "difficult child" who not only is slow to adapt but often displays an intense and negative mood (Carey & McDevitt, 1995, pp. 12–13). Understanding a young child's temperament can often help a teacher assess the best approach in teaching the child.

Parents Can Provide Important Information When Trying to Understand a Child's Recent Changes in Behavior or Motivation Around Schoolwork

Often, changes in the home can impact a child's classroom performance: changes such as a parent moving out, a sibling recently sharing a bedroom, or the mother going to work. Any number of changes in the home environment can have both a negative as well as a positive impact on a child's classroom performance.

One parent, as an example, was approached by her child's preschool teacher because of her son's sudden outbursts and aggressive behaviors in the classroom. After hearing this information, the parent shared that his father had his truck route recently changed and he was gone during the week and was home only on the weekends. This important information helped the teacher understand the child's recent aggressive behaviors. She was able to advise the parent on ways to help her child deal with the change at home.

Parents Can Share With Their Child's Doctor Your Feedback on the Effectiveness of Their Child's ADHD Medication

Often, a medication needs to be adjusted, and your input and observations are very important to assure positive results. Communication with the doctor generally occurs through the parent from the teacher. However, a parent may want you to speak directly with the doctor, so you will need a release of information from the parent to discuss your observations. If connecting with the doctor directly is difficult, you can e-mail, mail, or fax your observations to the doctor's office.

Parents Often Are a Great Resource for Information on ADHD

Many parents of children with ADHD quickly become experts out of necessity and are eager to share what they have learned. They generally have read a number of books and articles or attended area support groups on ADHD, such as CHADD (Children and Adults with Attention-Deficit Disorders). They can provide valuable resources to a teacher to help him or her better understand how to teach a child with ADHD.

In conclusion, the parent is the third leg of the stool in assuring maximum treatment of an ADHD child: doctor, teacher, and parent (see Figure 8.1). If one leg is missing, the stool is not as stable or as strong. To the greatest degree possible, communicate regularly with the parents on their child's performance at school. See the parents as a resource to help you better work with their child. With few exceptions, the only difference between the methods used at home and those used in school is primarily in the focus of the target behaviors. Rather than doing assigned chores at home and complying with a parent's command, the child is asked to sit quietly at a desk or obey a teacher's command (Barkley, 1995).

RESPECT AND ACKNOWLEDGE THE CHALLENGES PARENTS FACE

Parents of children with ADHD are challenged daily by their children's behaviors. They often look to others, such as teachers, to help give them respite from frustration, guilt, and self-blame. Sometimes parents who envision that the teacher has a "cookbook" of answers may become frustrated with the teacher when the child's classroom behaviors continue to be a problem.

Often, parents of children with ADHD feel helpless in changing some of their child's behaviors at school and, when confronted by the teacher, may strike back with angry or accusatory words. A parent can develop a sense of "learned helplessness"—a feeling that no matter what they do, reward or punishment, nothing seems to work (Barkley, 1995, p. 98). The parents, struggling daily to help their child, may eventually believe that there is no way to stop the child's misbehaviors and, in frustration, cease trying. This presents a frustrating situation for teachers, who occasionally ask more of parents than they are willing, or able, to give.

Figure 8.1   Three-Legged System of Support

A teacher will sometimes bear the brunt of angry parents' frustration over their lack of success in changing their child's behavior. Parents generally know their child can be a challenge in any number of environmental settings. Angry parents, unfortunately, will vent their frustrations onto the teacher. The parent's frustration can sometimes become accusatory and judgmental. As a teacher of a child with ADHD, it is very important you recognize that this is a possibility. The following suggestions should help in your interactions with parents.

Parents Often Need as Much Encouragement and Support as Their Child

Parents need to feel you are listening and that you understand their challenges. As one parent commented in frustration to a teacher, "If I could,

I would! He is not being successful because of a lack of effort on my part!" Most parents have tried any number of interventions, and when this effort is not recognized or validated by the teacher, the parent can become impatient and get angry.

Try to See That the Anger Directed at You Often Represents the Parents' Frustration

In most cases, the anger that is directed at teachers comes out of the parents' frustration in not being able to successfully help their child. The teacher, unfortunately, hears the parent's harsh words and feels attacked. One teacher described a parent "getting red in the face, accusing her of purposely picking on her child, and threatening to go to the principal if she kept calling her at work." This parent had come to the end of her rope. This teacher was face to face with an angry parent who, out of frustration, was in a blaming, accusatory, and threatening mood.

When confronted with an angry parent, try to picture in your mind a time when you didn't feel listened to or felt powerless to change a situation—this sometimes helps temper the natural feeling of wanting to strike back or defend yourself. The parent's anger becomes more understandable, and you can be more sympathetic to his or her frustrations.

Listen to Parents' Words Without Becoming Judgmental

It is only natural to want to defend your actions when you feel unfairly accused by a parent. No one is beyond having feelings of anger or feeling unfairly blamed when confronted by an angry person. However, striking back with angry words or taking a defensive position often only escalates the situation.

Recommended Steps to Help a Parent Feel More Understood

1.   Stay calm and try to voice what you believe the parent is most upset about. "Ms. Stanley, if I understand you correctly, you feel I have been unfairly picking on Bobby. Is this correct?" This important first step assures that you accurately understand the parent's concerns. It also helps the parent stop and listen. You are not judgmental or defending yourself, but simply asking for clarification.

2.   Acknowledge the parent's feelings, and don't quickly dismiss his or her point of view. "If I were in your position, I would likely feel the way you feel." You are not necessarily agreeing with the parent, but acknowledging that from his or her position, you can understand his or her feelings on the matter.

3.   Present your position in a nonaccusatory manner—use "I" statements. Try not to put the parent in a position where he or she feels blamed or responsible. Their child is responsible for his or her behavior, not the parent. A parent can be very helpful in tempering a child's actions at times, but the parent is not the child.

Suggested Ways to Share Your Concerns

1.   When the teacher says, "I thought you were going to talk with Danny? He's still not wanting to settle down at naptime," the parent often hears, "I am blaming you again." It's best to present your concerns as an "I" statement. Your goal is to get the parent's cooperation and involvement. "I know Danny has difficulty settling down to nap. I was wondering if we both spoke with him about ways he can quietly entertain himself during naptime, would it help?" The first statement puts the parent on the defensive, whereas the second statement presents the teacher's concern, but is not accusatory. The parent hopefully would feel less blamed and more open to suggestions or questions by the teacher.

2.   When the teacher says, "He still is not remembering to ask me before getting out of his seat," the parent may think, "I guess she thinks I didn't hear her the last time she brought this problem up." It's best to phrase a concern as an "I" statement and one that shows empathic feelings: "I become impatient with Danny forgetting to ask my permission before getting out of his seat; however, I know he doesn't always do it on purpose. What are some strategies you use at home?" The teacher presents his or her concern to the parent, but lets the parent know he or she understands that Danny sometimes forgets to ask because he is a child with ADHD. The teacher is also asking for the parent's suggestions, which may elicit some positive ways to address the teacher's concern. By presenting the concern in an empathic tone, a teacher is more likely to get positive feedback and cooperation from the parent. An alienated parent is less likely to listen or want to help.

Let Parents Know That Their Support Is Needed

Most parents are eager to help if they are asked; however, they can be as frustrated with their child at times as the teacher can. They need your recognition that they may not have all the answers. Once a parent feels needed, a teacher will often find the angry parent becoming a helpful parent who is more understanding of the teacher's position. Words that reach out to a parent's strengths and knowledge, not words that point out their failings, are best. Following are a few examples of this.

- "Ms. Andrew, I know you have learned a lot about what works best to get Sally to look at you when asking her a question. What do you recommend I do?"
- "Eric gets angry so quickly when I ask him to stop playing in his desk. What do you do that helps him not get angry so quickly?"
- "Bobby doesn't like to write out his letters. I know it must be quite a chore, but it's important he practice. Would you help him with his letters at home?"

In conclusion, the parent who feels listened to is generally more receptive to advice and cooperation. Positive communication between a teacher and parent often takes time, but the rewards are worth the time.

CRITICISM IS THE LEAST EFFECTIVE METHOD FOR CHANGE

Teachers may find that parents of children with ADHD can be hypersensitive to unsolicited input or recommendations. After experiencing many negative interactions with outside caretakers, a parent can become defensive and may turn a deaf ear to a teacher's suggestions on better ways to parent his or her child.

The parents sometimes see the teacher as being one more person at the end of a long list of well-intentioned people who have given their opinion on best practices in raising their child. A teacher's intent may be sincere, but the parent sometimes sees the advice as criticism. What can a teacher do?

Recognize that constructive change comes out of positive relationships, not textbooks or quick recipes you hear on the radio. It's very important to maintain a positive relationship with the parents so they are receptive to your suggestions or questions. Any recommendations you offer to the parent will be received more positively if the parent feels you care about his or her child or are understanding of his or her challenges. The parent will be more receptive to listening to tips or reading handouts you recommend on positive discipline, for example, if you have a positive relationship with the parent.

Be Sure to Point Out to the Parents Positive Choices Their Child Made In Class

It is natural when challenged by a student to speak with the child's parent about his or her disruptive or aggressive behaviors. In fact, most parents want to know if their child is misbehaving. However, it is also important to point out to the parents their child's positive choices, not just his or her bad choices. If the parents only hear negative reports, they sometimes become defensive and argumentative.

E-mail or Call Parents When the Child Has a Good Day

Calling or e-mailing parents about their child's good choices is very important. In fact, it often can be one of your most effective interventions in establishing ongoing positive and cooperative communication with a parent of a child with ADHD. Parents of children with ADHD often only hear from teachers when things are going badly. One parent, in a moment of honesty, commented: "I avoid answering the phone or I screen my calls during school hours until I have the emotional strength to deal with the school." This parent knew this was wrong and potentially dangerous, but after an unending series of negative calls from her child's school, she was at her wit's end.

E-mailing or calling parents to report positive steps or choices their child made that day can go a long way in giving the parent the strength to both answer the phone and to listen to you when their child has not had such a good day.

Let Parents Know Their Child Is Welcomed in Your Classroom

Parents of a child with ADHD can come to feel that their child is seen generally as a pest and is not welcomed by the teacher. This is especially the case for the extremely hyperactive and impulsive child who can frustrate even the most understanding teacher. Consequently, it is very important that teachers take the time and effort to verbalize to the parent positive statements about the affected child. One preschool teacher made it part of her daily lesson plan to speak with each parent when the child was dropped off and let the parent know her child was welcomed. A second-grade teacher pointed out to the parent of a child with ADHD how her child's high energy made him a great ball monitor at recess. Another teacher had one child with ADHD pass out math worksheets and made sure the parent knew how helpful this was to her. A little effort and time put toward "welcoming" statements can go a long way in helping the parents feel their child is welcomed in your classroom. In conclusion, when you have established a positive relationship with a parent, you will find that the parent will be more receptive to your suggestions and recommendations. Trust is the fuel that drives the engine of change.

ADHD AS AN "EXCUSE"

Teachers at workshops or staff meetings often mention that a parent will use ADHD as an excuse for their child's bad behavior or performance in school. Keep in mind that parents don't start out thinking that everything their child does is related to his or her diagnosis. In fact, most parents recognize that their child's diagnosis should not be seen as an excuse or "get out of jail free" card. Parents know that if their child hits another child in class out of anger or yells at the teacher, they will get in trouble.

So Why Do Teachers Sometimes Feel a Parent Is Using ADHD as an Excuse?

A teacher will sometimes hear parents say:

- He can't help running around during circle time or talking out during quiet reading time because he has ADHD.
- He doesn't mean what he says when he's angry; he is diagnosed with ADHD and can't help it.
- It's not fair he has to stay in from recess because he doesn't hear the bell to come in; he is diagnosed with ADHD and doesn't pay attention.
- He has ADHD, so why are you punishing him for forgetting to turn in his homework?
- If you knew anything about ADHD, you wouldn't be sending him to the principal's office all the time for talking in class.

As a teacher, you may have heard these or other similar comments and others as well. When teachers hear comments like these, they sometimes think the parent is excusing the child's behavior and not holding the child responsible. A teacher will comment that the parents are "enabling their child," not helping him or her learn ways to be more responsible. The teacher can come to feel that the parent is not supporting them or helping the child— a lose-lose situation.

Two factors that can contribute to this perception are:

1. The teacher viewing the parent's position as an "excuse" and not the parents' attempt to explain their child's behaviors. Often, parents aren't asking the teacher to be accepting of their child's behaviors, but are asking the teacher to acknowledge that their child's diagnosis is a contributing factor in his or her decision making.

2. There can develop a genuine misunderstanding of purpose and goals between the parent and teacher. What the teacher sees as an enabling behavior may often be perceived by the parents as an attempt to explain their child's behavior.

It's important, therefore, that both teacher and parent find common understanding.

HELPING PARENTS SEPARATE ENABLING FROM SUPPORTIVE DECISIONS

The teacher can be an important person in helping the parent separate enabling behavior from supportive choices. Parents are often conflicted by their child's problem ADHD behaviors. The dilemma presented to parents is one of trying to balance what the parents know society expects in terms of following rules with the recognition that their child's difficult behavior is often the consequence of his or her disorder and is not always willful or under his or her complete control. Most parents do not want to make excuses for their child, but are in constant turmoil over when he or she should or shouldn't be disciplined.

Parents know that when their child hits another child at school, he or she may be sent to the principal's office or even sent home. They understand that their child needs to know there are consequences for aggressive behaviors in school. Most parents do not accept aggressive behavior or see themselves making excuses, but can still ask themselves "He has ADHD—why discipline him for being impulsive?" Consequently, they may excuse the child's behavior, knowing full well that society does not tolerate these kinds of behavior.

Suggestions to help a parent not be enabling:

- Try to appreciate the difficulty a parent is presented by his or her child's ADHD behaviors. Children with ADHD can be challenging, often on a daily basis.
- Remind the parents that enabling behavior allows their child to believe he or she is not responsible because the child has ADHD. Let the parent understand that you recognize that their child has a disorder, but that he or she still needs to be held responsible for his or her behaviors. "I know Jason is impulsive, but when he runs in the classroom, it can be dangerous. I will need to put him in his seat when he starts running."
- Voice to the parent that children with ADHD, like unaffected children, need adults to help them find better ways to control their impulsiveness. "Ms. Thomas, I know it is difficult for Johnny to temper his impulsive behaviors, but he does better if I stay close to him when he becomes excited. He tells me it helps him to not run around as much if I remind him to slow down."
- Reinforce that children with ADHD, even when on medication, need to be educated about better ways to deal with problems.
- Provide regular feedback to the parents on the good choices their child made in class. The parents need to know when their child tempered his or her unhappy feelings and made a good decision. "Ms. Arnold, Eric made a good choice today during quiet reading time. He raised his hand

for permission before getting out of his seat. I let him choose his favorite sticker for raising his hand and asking if he could get out of his seat."

- Let the parents know you provide your students' positive incentives as well as discipline them when required. Their child is no different. He or she is rewarded and praised for good choices and disciplined when he or she makes poor choices.
- Support the parent when he or she has acknowledged and addressed the child's misbehaviors. "Thank you Ms. Thomas, I appreciate you speaking with Bobby about trying harder to not push in line when lining up for recess. He tells me you are practicing lining up at home. I know practicing at home will help him do better at school."
- Provide to the parent a list of books or handouts on ADHD. Education on ADHD is the most important intervention a parent can make in helping him or her to not be enabling (recommended books and Web sites are listed in Resource D, "Recommended Books for Teachers," and Resource E, "Useful Web Sites").

The teacher should frame the child's ADHD behaviors not as the child's problem, the parent's problem, or the teacher's problem, but as a challenge that needs to be addressed so the child can find more success. When parents see themselves as part of the solution where they are in concert with the teacher, success has a greater chance of being realized. Success doesn't mean the child's ADHD behaviors will go away. It does mean that many of the child's ADHD behaviors will become more manageable and, equally important, that the parent and teacher will be on the same page and the "blame" word will not long be on the table.

WHEN IT SEEMS A CHILD MIGHT HAVE ADHD

When is it appropriate to let parents know that you think their child might have ADHD? This is a very important question and must be handled with sensitivity. You have an important role to play in the evaluation of a student who may have ADHD. An affected child spends a large part of the day at school, and his or her teacher can compare the child's behavior with other students of similar age and gender. Physicians often perceive the teacher's observations as more balanced than those of the parents because teachers see such a large number of children and they are often more aware of aberrant behaviors. The parents generally have only siblings, cousins, or neighborhood children with whom to compare their child's behavior. Your advice is important and valued by physicians, psychologists, and other professionals who work with children outside the school setting.

You may ask, "What then can I say to parents about my suspicions that their child may have ADHD?" The following recommendations should help.

Don't attempt to label or tell a parent his or her child has ADHD. Educators are not qualified or licensed to diagnose a child with a medical or psychological disorder. Any diagnosis must be left up to a qualified person licensed or trained in neurological or psychological disorders. This person doesn't necessarily have to be a physician, but it is advisable that a physician be involved in any diagnosis of ADHD.

When talking to a parent about your concerns, be sensitive to the parent's reaction. No parent wants to hear disturbing news about his or her child. Parents often initially react with disbelief or anxiety that may present itself as anger, blame, or denial. You may be the recipient of their anger, so prepare your reactions. You may want another professional familiar with the child present to give you support.

Share your concerns in a private and nonthreatening space, not in a moment of frustration or anger. What you have to tell the parent is very important. You may want to set up an appointment with the parent ahead of time indicating you have something important to share. Make sure you block off enough time on your school calendar to answer questions or concerns from the parent.

Be clear about your concerns. When you share concerns with parents, give concrete examples to help clarify them. You are discovering some serious observations, and the parent will want examples or situations to support your assertion. Talk about behavior observed and stay away from labeling.

Be honest. A large part of your effectiveness in communicating with the parents will be the trust they have in you. Let the parents know why you requested a conference about their child. You can say, for example, "I wanted to talk with you about Bobby's behaviors. Some are really affecting his interactions with other children, such as _____. Have you noticed any of these behaviors at home? When I talk with him about them here in school, he does not seem able to change them. If he is not able to control these behaviors, then it's not fair for me to ask him to change them. I wonder if he might need more help, beyond what you are currently giving him, or what you might be able to give him. Perhaps you may want to talk with your family physician, to see if there might be something more that we can do together."

Share your concerns in a positive and constructive manner. A diagnosis of ADHD is not simple and often requires close communication between the parent, teacher, and doctor. Your first responsibility and task will be to communicate clearly with the parent, and by following some of the suggestions outlined here, you should find it more comfortable and less stressful for all parties involved.

If you do not have a good relationship with the parent, but still feel that the parent needs to be informed, ask someone else to be the messenger. It could be another teacher or the school counselor, school psychologist, or principal. It is important that the person observes the student a few times if he or she is going to talk about your concerns. The person can give credence to and validate your observations or suggest other possibilities for the child's behaviors.

Accept a parent's rejection of your concerns. Parents may initially not be open to your observations and feel you are wrong in your assessment. It this is the case, you still have done an important service for the child. The parent may later revisit your suggestions; consequently, even if your observations are not immediately accepted, you have planted the seed for later follow-up by the parent. Parents may initially reject the possibility that their child may have ADHD, but later in his or her schooling, reconsider this possibility. Your words and observations will ring in the parent's ear.

WHEN PARENTS DON'T DISCLOSE THAT THEIR CHILD IS TAKING MEDICATION

Teachers will sometimes only hear after the fact that a child was started on medication. Parents do not always share that their child is on medication for ADHD. Consequently, sometimes a teacher will be heard complaining, "Why didn't the parent let me know?"

Parents often feel uncomfortable disclosing that their child is on medication for ADHD. Unfortunately, medicating children for a mental disorder, such as ADHD, is still controversial and not fully embraced by our society. Consequently, parents withhold from teachers that their child is on medication "out of fear they will be criticized," as one parent shared.

Sometimes a parent is told by the doctor not to tell the teacher their child is on medication. A doctor may not be completely convinced the child has ADHD and wants to see if the teacher reports a significant change in the child's behavior after being placed on medication. More common, however, is the parents wanting to "test" and see if the teacher reports a real change in their child's behaviors. Parents often are not comfortable with their child being on medication and want to discover whether "it makes that big of a difference." As one parent reported, "If I tell the teacher Cody is on medication, she will just tell me he is better just because he's on medication." This parent, like many parents of children with ADHD, was manifesting her mixed feelings about medicating her child. It is not an easy decision parents make when deciding to put their child on medication, and it can often bring with it great trepidation.

A parent can also have great guilt around putting their child on medication. Parents may falsely conclude that their child's diagnosis is somehow their fault as a parent, either because they gave their child bad genes or because they have done something wrong in raising their child. This guilt tends to increase when the parent is asked to approve subjecting their child to what the parent might perceive as a potentially dangerous medication. The parent not only is confronting the stigma associated with a mental diagnosis, but the situation is now compounded by the idea that, as several parents have confided, "Something must really be wrong if the doctors think the child needs medication." A parent often needs time to adjust to this new and sometimes frightening intervention.

Broaching Medication With a Parent

When suspecting one of your students may have been placed on medication for ADHD, it's important that you address this observation with the parent in a sensitive manner. Recognizing some of the previous observations, it's important you gain the parents' trust so they are more open about their child's treatment. Your feedback to the parent and doctor on the medication's effectiveness is very important.

If parents have not disclosed that their child has started on medication, you should respect the parents need for privacy. Medicating a child is a very private matter and should be respected. You don't need to ask whether the child is on medication, but rather focus on giving the parents feedback on their child's behavior during the week. You can say, for example, "Cindy has been able to stay more focused this week" or "Cindy is a little more focused, but still has a difficult time during desk work." This information can give support to the parents about their decision to medicate or not medicate their child. Generally, after a period of time, parents will find the strength to share with their child's teacher that their child has been placed on medication for ADHD.

When the parent decides to share, encourage the parent to allow you to communicate with the doctor. The child is in your classroom for a good part of the day, and your feedback on the medication effectiveness is very important. Without your feedback, the doctor is less informed when measuring the effectiveness of the medication. (See Chapter 7 for information on what's helpful for teachers to share with doctors.)

Teachers are an important support to parents. Parents look to teachers for advice on any number of matters related to their child's education. An important component for some children with ADHD is medication. Open communication between the parent and teacher around this important intervention is an important component toward improving a child's educational and social-emotional development in school. Therefore, how teachers communicate with parents around this sensitive area is critical in a child's school success.

REGULAR COMMUNICATION IS CRITICAL

Even more so than with unaffected children, teachers need to communicate on a regular basis, sometimes daily, with the parent. Both preschool and early school-age children require close communication and monitoring between the parent and teacher. With preschool and early school-age children, a parent is instrumental in providing the teacher with new information that can affect a child's performance at school, such as changes in routine or other stressors in the home. Stressors can come from any number of situations, such as the child having a bad morning dressing before coming to school, the child being privy to parents' fighting, new sleeping arrangements, or a grandparent leaving the home after an extended visit. Any changes in a young child's home or school setting can cause additional stress on a child.

A kindergarten teacher shared that she didn't change her hairdo for at least six months after the beginning of school because she found it caused the children too much anxiety. Young children generally do best when routines are regular and there are not too many changes in their day.

Three, Two, One

We have found that one effective way to check on an affected child's readiness for the school day is to ask the parent when dropping their child off for school: "On a scale of three to one, how was your child's morning before coming to school?" ("Three" indicates good behavior with few problems, "two" indicates fair behavior, and "one" indicates poor behavior.) If the parent is not available when his or her child is dropped off at school, the parent can write the number on a sheet of paper for the teacher to read. If the parent reports a two or one, the teacher will know the child may need special monitoring or attention. Sometimes, depending on a child's maturity, the child can use this number scale to let the teacher know how he or she feels. With a difficult child who says "one," it is often helpful for the child to have time alone until he or she feels better. Often, after a short period of time alone, the child is ready to join in group activities or start on the school assignments.

E-mail or Telephone

It's often helpful for the teacher to connect with the parent regularly on the child's day by phone or e-mail. When communicating with the parent, it is important that you are calm. Make a point to call or e-mail when observing progress, not only when the child presents disruptive behaviors in class. Sometimes with a challenging child, it's hard to find something good, but it is very important that you try. One teacher jokingly shared that with one child, it was so hard on some days for her to find something nice to say to the child, that she sent him to the teacher next door to be complimented.

Frankly, some children with ADHD can be so disruptive to a classroom that a teacher is at times challenged to find something good to say about the child to the parent. Please forgive yourself if you have experienced these thoughts. Two qualities above all make a good teacher when teaching difficult children: the ability to forgive oneself and learning to say, "I am sorry." Both learned skills are necessary for peace of mind when teaching children.

Notes Home

Notes to a parent on his or her child's behavior should be short and not judgmental. As mentioned before, criticism is the least effective form for change. Teachers shouldn't say, for example, "Ms. Stewart, I thought you said you were going to check his backpack. He again forgot to bring back his homework. Please call me." A more positive way to address this concern would be, as an example, to write a short note or call the parent, saying: "Ms. Stewart, I put a brown manila folder in Eric's backpack. You can use this to put all his homework in before coming to school. I should have thought about this when I last spoke with you." You have given the parent a gentle reminder but also provided an intervention that may be helpful to the parent. It may be true that the parent is inconsistent in checking his or her child's backpack, but judgmental remarks only distance and anger a parent and don't help bring about positive changes.

A note put in a child's cubby or in his or her backpack can be an effective form of communication with the parent. It can be used as a gentle reminder, reinforcement of a parent's good effort, or tips on working with a homework assignment.

Teachers can find any number of Web sites that will provide resources to help generate monitoring and management activities. You will find suggested Web sites for teachers listed in Resource E, "Useful Web Sites."

SUMMARY

When teachers view the parent as an important resource whose input is valued and listened to, they find more success in working with a child with ADHD. Managing and teaching very young children with ADHD can be very challenging, and parents' support and involvement is often necessary. Parent communication that is built on respect and empathy can be your most important intervention when teaching children with ADHD. A parent whose concerns are listened to is more receptive to a teacher's recommendations and that parent is more likely to be a partner with the teacher in the education of his or her child.

Taking Care of Yourself

9

No job is more satisfying than teaching children; however, no job in education is more demanding or stressful than is teaching. Teaching requires total focus and attention while in the classroom. Teachers are responsible not only for the education of children under their care, but for their safety as well. The principal and other support staff in schools have the luxury of taking five—not the teacher. Children under a teacher's care require his or her total attention. Teachers can't let personal discomforts or outside stresses be a distractor while children are under their care. The teacher's focus and attention on the children need to be 100%!

Consequently, teaching can put great stress on a teacher's physical and emotional well-being. It's important for teachers to find ways to take care of themselves, both physically and emotionally.

RECOGNIZING THE SIGNS OF STRESS

Stress is a normal part of life for everyone, and when we become highly stressed, our body gives us signs that we can use to help us recognize when the stress is not healthy. When very stressed or anxious, for example, our pulse can quicken, we might feel flushed, and adrenaline readies us for "fight or flight." Unfortunately, when highly stressed or upset, we can react impulsively and later regret our actions.

Stress might build up when hearing that a parent is in the office wanting to talk with you about suspending his or her child or just discovering that your preschool child with ADHD has for the fifth time hit another child with a toy. Stress will come in all shapes, colors, and sizes; it's up to you to find ways to make it manageable.

SUGGESTED WAYS TO LOWER STRESS

1.   Begin to see the child's behaviors as symptomatic of his or her disorder. Sometimes, after repeated conflicts or disappointments with the child, it's not unreasonable to want to personalize the child's actions. "If he really cared or wanted to listen, he wouldn't need to ask me over and over again what he needed to do!" Your perception of the child's behavior can influence the level of personal stress stemming from the child's inattentive and impulsive behaviors.

2.   Recognize that "self-talk" about the child can influence your stress level. As an example, if a driver cuts in front of you on the highway, you can choose to shout and yell, or "reframe" the driver's actions by telling yourself, "He must be in a hurry because he might have heard that his child was seriously injured at school." Even though you recognize that this might not be the case, it still can help with controlling your anger level as well as your stress level. You may still be a little upset, but not as much as you would be if you saw the driver's behavior as rude and selfish. When we think negative, distressing, and critical thoughts, we increase our negative emotions. Try it, you may be surprised.

3.   Acknowledge that not all problems need to be fixed right away. Some problems are important to address, but not urgent. Behaviors of marginal importance such as a child putting his knees up on his chair while working, making noises during quiet time, or forgetting to turn in his homework are important to address, but they are not a safety matter, nor do they always require your immediate attention. You can take a moment to reflect on the behavior and sometimes ignore a behavior if not too disruptive. You don't need to fix all problems right way.

4.   There is no shame in asking for help if you have reached your limit with an affected child. You can ask the teacher next door if he or she will take the child at times when you feel you have no more patience. It's only reasonable, even for the best of teachers, to become overly stressed with a difficult child. Have a plan in place for moments when you need a break from the child. Many times, it's only for a short period of time. One teacher would send the child to the office with a sealed envelope to drop off, knowing that there were only empty binder papers inside. Office staff, prepared ahead of time by the teacher, would thank the child and send him back to his classroom. This simple intervention allowed the child to move around and redirect negative into positive behavior, and allowed the teacher to regroup herself.

5.   See the parents as important helpers in the education of their child. As discussed in Chapter 8, the parent can be your most important helper. Don't feel you need to go it alone. The parent can communicate with the child's doctor, reinforce activities you do in the classroom at home, and provide suggestions at times that can be helpful. However, your request for help needs to be framed not in anger, but caring words.

6.   You can only offer the opportunity for change, you cannot make change happen. Understand that there are many variables and reasons in explaining a child's behavior. Your classroom can be the best classroom environment for a child with ADHD to learn, but your sincere efforts cannot assure the child will always be successful. Sometimes children's behaviors are so significant or their learning challenges so paramount that they may require outside support and an educational placement more restrictive than your classroom can offer

7.   Measure your efforts as steps toward your goal and not as ends in themselves. When you see your efforts as important by themselves, you will be more capable of handling the disappointments when the child doesn't progress as much as you might have thought. Remember, ADHD is a disorder of performance, not ability. The child often knows what he or she needs to do, but struggles to do it consistently. Measure your successes by what you can control and not by those things you cannot control.

8.   Try to maintain a daily exercise routine at school (short walks during prep or lunch) or "no shop talk" time with a colleague. There is plenty of time for shop talk so make sure there is a time when it is "out of bounds." Focus on activities and discussions that are calming and don't bring additional stress to your school day.

9.   Last, we bring to work personal stresses from marital problems to medical concerns. It's important to recognize that outside stresses will affect your ability to deal with difficult children. Simple self-talk words, such as "I overreacted just now; it must be I am still upset with my daughter from this morning" can help. Verbalizing possible stressors helps identify unresolved conflicts or worries. No one is immune to stress, so if you can identify your outside stresses in your life, you are less likely to have them negatively impact your teaching day.

Self-care is an important goal and should not be minimized or put on the back burner in a teacher's workday. Self-care should include both physical as well as psychological interventions, from exercising regularly to finding self-calming words that help minimize daily stresses, not elevate them.

If your stressors seem overwhelming, it's important to speak with your doctor. Don't feel you need to go it alone.

Children with ADHD are not easy to teach or manage. They can bring great stress to a teacher's day, and it's important that teachers find ways to handle the associated stresses. We have attempted in our book to provide you guidance and suggestions that can make your teaching day with children with ADHD less stressful and more successful.

We can offer you helpful tips, but we cannot guarantee that you will take them to heart and implement them in your classroom. As the classroom teacher, you are the primary contact person in conveying compassion, understanding, respect, and interest in the needs of a child with ADHD. You should expect the best from the child, both behaviorally and academically; however, you also need to offer the necessary educational support for the child to be more successful. You can make an important difference in a child's development.

Even though teachers cannot prevent the underlying neurological impairment found in children with ADHD or fix bad parenting, they can do a better job preventing these impairments from causing academic and social failure. Teachers can be more effective in teaching these children better ways to control their impulses and emotions. Daniel Goleman (1995) suggests that schools can be more proactive in "schooling the emotions." Schools can partner with parents in helping affected children find better ways to deal with their emotions. "Emotional lessons" can merge naturally into daily academic curriculum. This is a daunting task, but for schools to meet the needs of difficult children such as these, they must see their role as beyond their traditional mission of teaching reading, writing, and arithmetic. "The larger design requires," in the words of Daniel Goleman (1995), "apart from any specifics of curriculum, using opportunities in and out of the class to help students turn moments of personal crisis into lessons of emotional competence" (p. 280).

In conclusion, sometimes the relationship between a teacher and the affected child can be a "good-enough" relationship, borrowing from Mark Karpel's (1994) description of couple relationships. Just as in marriages, periods of contentment can be disrupted by periods of extreme tension and discord. A good-enough teacher/child relationship is not problem free, but there should develop patterns of communication that help maintain a sense of fairness in the relationship.

We wish you the best of luck in working with your students with ADHD and encourage you to use this book as a resource to help you teach the child with ADHD. Hopefully, your newfound knowledge and confidence should shelter you from storms that come your way when teaching this unique and very special child.

Resources

Resource A

Recognizing ADHD in Preschool
and Primary Grades: Real Profiles

Teachers are generally resistant to accept labels for or to put labels on a child in their classroom. Most teachers don't look for or want to acknowledge a psychiatric diagnosis in a very young child. In fact, only a very small percentage of young children have serious psychiatric disorders. However, there are some children whose behavior is so difficult to manage, both at home and in school, that the parents need to bring their child to a mental health specialist for a formal evaluation. Some of these children will later be diagnosed with ADHD.

ADHD behaviors will often bring challenges, and sometimes heartache, to preschool and elementary school teachers. An affected child is not easy to teach or to manage. The following profiles are intended to help you identify and respond to children who manifest symptoms of ADHD in your classroom.

PRESCHOOL

When a child first enters preschool, he or she is involved, often for the first time, with a large group of children in a social and educational setting. Depending on the program, a child may be with large groups of children for either half a day or one full day. It is generally at this time that a preschool teacher will flag a child who is presenting behavioral, social, or educational challenges.

Diagnosing ADHD in preschool-age children is extremely difficult because very young children often manifest ADHD-like behaviors for any number of reasons. ADHD-like symptoms may stem from medical, cognitive-language, developmental, or other psychiatric conditions that can mimic true ADHD.

It is common for preschool children to present inattentive, hyperactive, and impulsive behaviors at different times of the day and across different environmental settings. Therefore, the key question that needs to be answered is whether the child's ADHD behaviors, when compared with other children his or her chronological age, are significantly interfering with his or her readiness for preschool, readiness to explore the world, and readiness to interact with others in a positive way. Thus, "it is the manner in which ADHD makes it difficult to do what is expected at a given age" that is assessed by professionals (Anastopoulos & Shelton, 2001, p. 46). If there are any doubts as to the level of severity or underlying causes, professionals generally are reluctant to diagnose a child with ADHD at this very young age.

The following vignettes describe two preschool children with ADHD. Brian presents a number of behavioral and language delays, which makes a definitive diagnosis of ADHD difficult at his young age. Rachel presents classic ADHD behaviors that are more representative of a preschooler appropriately diagnosed with ADHD.

Brian

Brian's parents first referred him for an assessment at 3 years, 11 months, because of great difficulty adjusting to daily activities in a private preschool childcare program. When observed in class by a therapist, Brian had great difficulty with focused and sustained attention for any extended period of time, especially when involved in age-appropriate classroom activities such as circle time and table work. He seemed not interested with group activities, even those that were interactive in scope and child-directed. He often was observed leaving a group activity and going off and doing something by himself.

Brian presented low frustration, regularly and stubbornly resisting when confronted or directed by staff to do something he didn't like to do. He would become noncompliant and oppositional and easily resort to temper tantrums or outbursts if pressed to comply. His parents reported that they were experiencing similar behavior at home. The developmentally normal statement "I can do it!" would escalate into intense battles at home, and the typical striving for independence became an intense battle for control.

The therapist discussed with Brian's parents her observations that Brian, in addition to displaying noncompliant and oppositional behaviors, also presented autistic-like behaviors, a possible auditory processing disorder, or ADHD.

Brian's parents reported to the therapist that he had been evaluated earlier for autism at three years of age by a regional center. His parents had received behavioral management training in the home for five months to address his behaviors, however, autism was later ruled out after further examination by an agency specializing in developmental disorders.

Even though Brian's expressive language seemed age appropriate, his difficulty complying with auditory directions raised the possibility that he had an auditory processing disorder. He did not seem to respond to auditory cues and had difficulty maintaining eye contact when spoken to directly by his teacher. Children with an auditory processing disorder have difficulty comprehending what is requested or asked of them. It is not a hearing difficulty, but a processing disorder. They can often be distracted by background sounds or noises and find it difficult to stay focused on or to remember a verbal request or presentation. They often misinterpret or have difficulty remembering oral directions and will be seen ignoring people, especially if engrossed in an activity. Children with an auditory processing disorder sometimes will have a diagnosis of ADHD or present behaviors similar to those associated with ADHD.

Brian's speech and language testing found significant delays in verbal comprehension, but ruled out an auditory processing disorder. Similar to his behavior at childcare, Brian presented oppositional and ADHD-based behaviors during his sessions at the university where he was tested and treated. The speech therapist provided ongoing, one-on-one reinforcement through a token system to improve his on-task and compliant behaviors. However, even with one-on-one attention, he made little eye contact initially with the speech therapist and resorted to intermittent noncompliant behaviors when he didn't want to participate. He showed some improvement in eye contact and noncompliance after six months of speech therapy, but still needed support in minimizing the ADHD and noncompliant behaviors.

Finally, Brian also presented delays in social development. His interactions with his peers found interactions suggestive of a child younger than his chronological age. He was unable to do cooperative play for any extended period of time. Cooperative play between peers requires some degree of means-end thinking and the ability to plan and work toward a goal. These tasks are often impaired in children with ADHD because of developmental delays in working memory. He was "driven by the moment" and unable to interact for any extended period of time with other children. He was unable to establish strong bonds with his classmates, which is normally reflected in prolonged bouts of joint play and cooperation. He had demonstrated only limited development in "parallel play," which is marked by similarity of the participants' actions and by their awareness of each other, despite relatively little direct exchange or turn taking. He seemed self-absorbed and only would interact for short periods of time in any meaningful manner. However, his parents reported that he was more interactive at home with his siblings or when his parents gave him one-on-one attention. This information suggested that some of his interactions with peers could be understood as "anxiety driven" in light of the fact that with his siblings and family he was more interactive.

During this period of time, Brian's parents had decided to remove him from his preschool because of continuing behavioral difficulties. However, he continued his speech and language sessions at the university.

In light of his developmental history and lack of progress in preschool, the therapist recommended that a child psychiatrist evaluate Brian and the parents ask for an Individualized Education Plan (IEP) to further evaluate his current abilities and development. The IEP would help identify Brian's short-term and long-term educational needs. His IEP would include goals and objectives that prescribe teaching accommodations and strategies that would support his education.

Psychoeducational and language testing found Brian to have average cognitive ability, but significant language delays. He was placed in a special day class for preschool communicative-handicapped children. He was diagnosed with ADHD by the psychiatrist and placed on medication. However, after presenting significant motor tics while on medication, he was taken off medication for his ADHD. His parents, however, continued to be given support through an ADHD parent-support group at the hospital.

Brian's diagnosis of ADHD is still being closely monitored by his doctor, and time should determine whether an ADHD diagnosis would continue to be appropriate for him. He continues to receive speech and language services through a communicative-handicapped classroom in kindergarten.

Rachel

Rachel came to the attention of the Head Start program mental health specialist because of her aggressive, noncompliant, and high-risk behaviors at the age of 4 years, 6 months. Rachel attended an all-day Head Start preschool program in a large, metropolitan school district.

Rachel's teachers described her as very active and reported that she would put herself and other children in the classroom at risk on a daily basis. Even with close monitoring, her teachers would find her jumping from tables, running into bookcases, and running away from staff when asked to come into the classroom. One time, she was observed spinning in circles on the classroom floor for no apparent reason. Her teachers reported that these behaviors occurred more often than not.

There had been a number of contacts with support staff and her parents; however, little progress was made even after numerous staff/parent meetings. Consequently, the staff made a referral to the program mental health specialist. After a number of observations, the therapist noted behaviors suggestive of ADHD. Rachel had great difficulty participating in circle time and would wander around the room, running from one area to another. Even after repeated reminders and redirection from staff, she could only comply for short periods of time before running off again to do something by herself.

During free time, she would interact with other children, but only for short periods of time, and generally the interactions were confrontational, with Rachel wanting to be in control. Children eventually began to distance themselves from her, not sure what to expect from moment to moment. Often, when she was observed trying to interact with another child, she would be taunting the child or would become quickly upset or frustrated if she didn't get her way. Staff often had to intervene or to remove her for short periods of time from interacting with a child or participating in a group activity.

Rachel especially had difficulty during table time when sharing and taking turns was important. She had great difficulty self-regulating her impulsive acts, such as taking toys away from another child without asking or not waiting her turn during share time. She would blurt out and interrupt other children when they were sharing. When staff intervened, she would become resistant and run away, goading the teacher to chase her. When caught, she would show little remorse for her behavior and seemed not to learn from her mistakes.

Naptime at school was an especially difficult time for Rachel. She rarely settled down to sleep, and even when given options such as quietly reading or playing with a toy, she would need constant one-on-one monitoring to keep her on her cot. When pressed by staff to stay on her cot or to sit quietly at a table, she often became oppositional and would run out the door or around the room.

Parents described similar behaviors at home. She would rarely nap as a toddler, and they had great difficulty taking her out to a restaurant or to the store. She would not stay close to her mother and would bolt away, running from one end of the aisle to the other. Sometimes the parents would describe having to run her down in the store as she darted around an aisle. At home, she was constantly on the go, and they had difficulty getting a babysitter to return after a "one-night experience."

Rachel was referred to an outside mental health specialist after a number of failed interventions at school and home. The parents and school staff were finding themselves exhausted and running out of ideas on how best to deal with this young child's behavior.

Rachel was diagnosed with ADHD by a psychiatrist and was placed on medication. Staff and parents saw immediate change for the better. She was more compliant, she was able to sit during circle time, and her interactions with staff and peers were more positive. Academically, prior to being placed on medication, she was behind in knowing her colors and numbers. After

Rachel was placed on medication, her teacher marveled at her quick progress in mastering these important concepts. Her parents talked about a significant change at home. She was able to settle down for bed at a reasonable time and to entertain herself more often without constantly interrupting her parents. Before being placed on medication, she often would not fall asleep until 10:30 or 11:00 at night and needed constant parental participation and supervision when playing alone or with her sister.

Medication seems to have helped put "brakes" on Rachel's impulsive and hyperactive behaviors. She was able to maintain more focused attention and consequently was able to make significant progress by the end of her preschool year. Without the added support of medication and the staff's better understanding of her behavior, this child would have been at risk when entering kindergarten. She presented classic ADHD-based behaviors and, with appropriate interventions, staff and her parents were able to maximize her social/emotional and academic development.

Reflection

Brian and Rachel present both similar and dissimilar profiles. Brian is a young child in whom ADHD is very difficult to diagnose definitively. He presents a number of developmental factors that contributed to his social/emotional development and inattention. Even though he clearly presents difficulties in inattention (focused and sustained attention) compared with his peers, he also is challenged by significant language delays.

Rachel, unlike Brian, is more representative of "clean ADHD." She presents classic ADHD symptoms with minimal associated conditions. High impulsivity and disinhibition trigger her aggressive and noncompliant behaviors—a pattern commonly seen in affected children. Her behaviors were significantly elevated compared with her classmates and were interfering in her social/emotional and academic development. Unlike Brian, she responded very positively to medication, which helped minimize her problematic behaviors, such as noncompliance and impulsivity. She is now able to interact with staff and peers in a more positive manner and has mastered the preschool curriculum important for kindergarten readiness.

KINDERGARTEN AND FIRST GRADE

A kindergarten and first-grade student with ADHD can present many behaviors similar to the preschooler; however, because academic and behavioral expectations are often more demanding, the child with ADHD can quickly find himself or herself in trouble.

Children are usually ready for kindergarten if they can leave their parents without too much fuss, and if they can follow simple directions and rules, play cooperatively with other children and respect their possessions, and resolve conflicts without always running to the teacher. A child should be able to talk in complete sentences and tell a story; work independently for at least 5 minutes and listen to a story for 10 minutes; recognize shapes, colors, and rhymes; and use paints, paste, and crayons. These activities measure a child's development in a number of neuropsychological processes: sensory-motor, auditory processing, attention and impulse control, and memory.

In the first grade, children not only are being asked to interact with others in socially appropriate ways, but to master curriculum that in the past was introduced at later stages in a child's educational development. The "top-down" process of educating children is largely driven, as one writer suggests, by the need to develop an increasingly skilled workforce and not with the child's best educational and social/emotional interests in mind (Porter, 2002). Unfortunately, as Louise Porter (2002) notes, the "fact that many young children can learn an academic curriculum does not mean that they should" (p. 57). Porter goes on to write that

> children's dispositions and in-depth understanding can be harmed by confronting them too early with tasks whose content and processes are too demanding, that when children are deprived of physical play in favor of academic work, neural pathways in the brain that are essential for academic success cannot be strengthened. (p. 57)

The educational trend in the United States of introducing higher level curriculum at lower grades can be especially challenging for children with ADHD, who often are developmentally younger than their chronological age. An affected child who has difficulty sitting for an extended period of time, gets bored quickly, and is more impatient and impulsive than the unaffected child can find the day-to-day activities in a kindergarten and first-grade classroom very difficult.

Like Brian and Rachel, the children you'll read about next are diagnosed with ADHD.

Tyler

Tyler, 5 years 3 months, entered kindergarten with a history of delays in social development and was described both by his parents and by his kindergarten teacher as highly emotional, impulsive, and inattentive. He would become upset quickly, often crying and needing a lot of support from his teacher to regroup.

Tyler was a premature baby weighing 5 pounds, 3 ounces, at birth. He was colicky and had a history of ear infections. He always had difficulty settling down at night, and many times when he was a toddler, he would be found wandering the house after the family had gone to bed. It would sometimes take one to two hours for him to fall asleep after being put to bed. When he was awakened in the morning for school, he often was tired and irritable. He was always on the go and was accident prone. He would require very close monitoring when in public, often running away from his parents in a store or parking lot. Even after many reprimands and reminders, he "didn't seem to learn." He continued to wet his bed at night and during the day would occasionally soil his pants.

When Tyler entered preschool, he had great difficulty adjusting to the schedules and routines. He quickly came to the attention of the staff because of his impulsive behaviors. He would grab toys from a child without asking, walk away during circle time and go play with a toy, and swing or throw objects carelessly in the classroom, and he often required one-on-one "shadowing" by a staff member when on fieldtrips. Free time was especially difficult because staff would find him in isolated play because other children were guarded around him and avoided his company because of his behaviors. Coupled with his impulsive and hyperactive behaviors, Tyler presented significant difficulty in self-regulating his emotions. He would quickly become angry or upset, leading to long periods of crying. His mother sometimes would be called to help him calm down. Staff and parents were concerned that his crying spells had escalated and his crying was a reaction to his feelings of isolation from peers and being reprimanded by staff on a regular basis at school.

The parents referred Tyler to be evaluated by a child psychologist shortly before entering kindergarten because of his continuing difficulties. In light of his developmental history and elevated impulsive and hyperactive behaviors, the child psychologist referred Tyler to a psychiatrist. He was diagnosed with ADHD and put on medication shortly after school started. His kindergarten teacher reported his impulsive and hyperactive behavior had diminished since he was placed on medication; however, he still continued to have "crying spells." His crying spells, however, diminished after the second quarter in school, perhaps because he was receiving support from a number of resources. The family was seeing a therapist specializing in ADHD to better understand his disorder and to find more positive ways to deal with his behaviors. The school was in contact with the therapist and had put in place some recommended interventions.

Tyler, even on medication, continued to need accommodations at school. He still had difficulty with paper-and-pencil tasks, following teacher directions, and positive peer interactions. His teacher, parents, and therapist coached him on better ways to make and to keep friends. The medication coupled with behavioral modification was helping his behavioral challenges; however, he still needed support with academic tasks, such as "starting and stopping" and transitioning from one subject area to another.

The parents, because of Tyler's young age, discussed with the doctor the idea of taking Tyler off medication and working with the therapist on behavioral modification and educational accommodations to address his behavioral and academic challenges. The doctor concurred and Tyler was taken off his medication; however, because of his young age, his impulsivity and hyperactive behaviors were still very pronounced, and he was put back on medication after a 10-week trial period off medication.

Tyler's difficulties stemmed in part from his untreated ADHD, but now treated, Tyler's prospects are good. He has a supportive family, close monitoring by his doctor, and an understanding by the school about his specific challenges. His parents reported that by the end of his kindergarten year, he had made new friends and had a more positive outlook. They talked again about wanting to take him off medication at a later date, but not in the near future.

Zackary

Zackary was diagnosed with ADHD in the middle of his kindergarten year. His parents were against putting him on medication and were trying alternative treatments when he entered the first grade. They had investigated a number of treatments, from diet to vitamin supplements. They had found minimal success with these treatments, but were still against medicating their son for ADHD at his young age.

Zackary, in the first grade, had difficulty sitting at his desk and presented many fidgety and distracting behaviors. He would sit up with both feet on his seat, crawl under his desk, and fall off his chair from time to time. He would become highly distracted by external movements or noises in class—a child walking down the aisle, someone sharpening a pencil, or a student being helped by the teacher. His teacher had to give him verbal reminders throughout the day to help him stay on task. Like many affected children, he attended to everything around him—except what he needed to attend to.

Zackary did not display significant impulsivity, but more moderate hyperactive and inattentive behaviors. He was fidgety, but generally compliant. Consequently, he made friends easily and was not in trouble too often at school. He especially had difficulty with inattention in a number of areas that affected his day-to-day classroom performance. He had difficulties with focus; sustained, divided, and selective attention; and vigilance, all of which impacted his daily school performance. He would be observed daydreaming and not attending to the teacher's directions or assigned lessons.

He would be focusing on other activities instead of what was being talked about (focus attention). He had great difficulty remaining on a task long enough to sufficiently complete that task (sustained attention) and had difficulty listening and doing something at the same time (divided attention). Someone walking down the aisle to the front of the room or a child sharpening a pencil (selective attention) would distract Zackary. Unlike unaffected children who may be distracted by these activities, he was unable to get back to his assigned work without teacher reminders. Last, he had difficulty waiting for the teacher to complete her directions before starting on an assignment (vigilance, or readiness to respond).

Zackary's school performance also suggested a possible learning disability, but because of his young age, formal testing was delayed. His teacher reported that his sensory-motor processing was delayed and that it was affecting his writing performance. Sometimes, maturation will correct concerns around this cognitive process. Zackary, like many ADHD children, also presented cognitive deficits in working memory, which can affect reading readiness.

Probably the most problematic area for Zackary was his difficulty in "remembering to remember." Like many affected children, he would forget to turn in his papers, put his name on his paper, and line up when the recess bell sounded. Homework was a challenge too. It would take him three times longer to finish a short homework assignment than expected for his age. This was especially the case when paper-and-pencil tasks were involved. He would often not remember to take home his worksheets and, when completing the homework, often failed to remember to turn the homework in the next day in class. Unlike his peers, considerable effort and reminders from his teacher were needed to assure the homework was completed and turned in.

To date, Zackary is generally doing well in school; however, as he moves up in grades, in which independent and more self-directed work is required, he may be more challenged by his ADHD behaviors. In terms of getting along with others, his social skills were intact, and he was not oppositional or highly impulsive. He made friends easily and was generally a happy kid. His suspected learning disability may become more problematic as he advances in grades.

Reflection

Tyler is a young boy who is continuing to be monitored at school for his ADHD behaviors. He is a child who may be vulnerable to secondary disorders, such as a mood or anxiety disorder, as he progresses in his grades. His ADHD symptoms have been minimized through medication, but his parents would like him to start off the new school year without medication. They recognize and accept his diagnosis, but hope that maturation can minimize some problematic behaviors, and through formal entitlements, like Section 504, he will continue to be provided important classroom accommodations. Tyler is a child who may not need medication as part of his treatment as he progresses in his grades. He has a lot of protective factors such as positive peer relationships, parent support, and openness to classroom accommodations by school staff.

Zackary, like Tyler, is a child who continues to have difficulty with inattention and distractibility. His parents continue to be opposed to medication, and the school is continuing to try ways to address his ADHD behaviors. Like Tyler, Zackary has good peer relationships and is not oppositional. He does present concerns for a learning disability in sensory-motor processing; however, maturation may correct this cognitive processing delay. If it continues to be a concern, formal assessment would be recommended in the second grade. As written work becomes more demanding, he may need accommodations in written language.

SECOND AND THIRD GRADE

When affected children enter the second or third grade, they often find school more challenging. By this age, children are expected to have better mastered classroom rules, playground behaviors, and enhanced study skills. However, children who need to move around and who get bored easily with routine activities are not good candidates for success in the average American classroom.

Many of those ADHD traits that are problematic for school-age children are most pronounced in the lower grades: hyperactivity, impulsivity, and inattention. Like the kindergarten or first-grade student, school expectations and activities often challenge the affected second- and third-grade student. Many students continue to be challenged by classroom routines, recess, and appropriate social skills. In addition to having to master tasks such as lining up at recess, remembering to turn in assigned papers, and starting and stopping when told, the affected child is challenged by additional school tasks: homework, standardized testing (SAT 9), and more writing activities.

The cognitive style of the affected child is qualitatively different from that of most people. His or her tendency to move from one thought to another and from one project to another without completion creates challenges in the school setting. He or she can be inattentive one moment and be overly focused on an activity and thought the next (Hallowell & Ratey, 1994).

Andy

Andy, a second-grade student, was diagnosed with ADHD in the middle of the first grade. His parents had put him on medication for a short time during the first grade, but decided to take him off to see what would happen the following year. They had recently moved and were anxious to see if he would do better in a new school and with a new teacher. Andy's parents, when enrolling him in his new school, did not share his diagnosis with the principal or classroom teacher. They wanted to wait and see and felt that talking to the teacher would "prejudice her against Andy."

Andy's teachers reported that his first week of school was problematic. The first week of school can be an adjustment for any child. Enrolling in a new school, coming off of an extended vacation, or adjusting to a new routine can cause adjustment behaviors in any young child. Consequently, staff initially attributed his hyperactive and inattentive behaviors to these changes. After three weeks of school and seeing no improvement, the teacher telephoned the parents for a meeting to address his behaviors. At the meeting, his parents reported for the first time that Andy was diagnosed with ADHD. They were apologetic to the teacher for not informing her of his diagnosis and confessed they had wanted to wait and see and make sure the diagnosis was correct. Andy presented classic ADHD behaviors in class. He had great difficulty transitioning from one activity to another, getting started and stopping when asked, and staying seated during class work, and he made disruptive sounds at his desk while working.

Recess was often difficult too. He would be playing and forget to line up when the bell rang and would quickly become angry if reprimanded or upset with another child. He would impulsively strike out at other children or bark back at teachers who tried to intervene. He had to be put on a modified recess schedule because of his behaviors. Andy's disposition was generally easygoing; however, when put in an unstructured and high-arousal state, such as recess, he could become violent and get out of control. He would find himself is serious trouble and would be teased by his classmates.

Andy was resistant to writing tasks, and it often took many reminders by his teacher to get him started and to stay with a writing task. His parents reported that even short writing assignments would "take an unreasonable amount of time" and create a "World War III" atmosphere at home. Such tasks, from spelling tests to worksheets, were more common in the second grade, and Andy became noncompliant and oppositional, which would bring negative attention from his teacher and parents.

Andy presented both ADHD behaviors and problems with completing writing assignments. Shortly into his third-grade year, Andy was again placed on medication for his ADHD and was identified with a learning disability in written language. He was provided accommodations through an IEP for his disability, and his parents regularly attended local CHADD meetings (a national support group for parents with children with ADHD—see Resource E for Web site) to help them better understand his disorder. They had moved from the bargaining stage to acceptance of his diagnosis. The school, parents, and doctor were working closely together to provide support for this young child.

Andy will need ongoing support as he advances in his grades, but he should find success because of his early treatment and educational support.

Timothy

Timothy is the last and most problematic case of a child with ADHD that we look at here. Timothy had presented problematic ADHD behaviors since a very young age. He was removed from preschool because of his aggressive and out-of-control behaviors. Preschool teachers write that he was noncompliant, violent toward staff and peers, and a risk to himself. After many interventions with little success, he was removed from the preschool program.

His parents noted that he was a "difficult infant," waking up in the morning irritable and generally in a "sour mood." He never napped and rarely slept through the night. He would awaken and wander the house. His parents had to lock the doors leading outside to assure his safety. As a toddler, his tantrums were extreme and often lasted 45 minutes to an hour. He would throw things, scratch, and bite, and he seemed indifferent to punishment or pain. He had to be taken to the emergency room on more than one occasion because of his impulsive behaviors. On one occasion, he had run out the front door and fell down the apartment stairs, breaking his arm in the fall. The parents noted that they were investigated by child protective services because of his history of multiple accidents.

When his parents were enrolling him for kindergarten, he became upset with having to wait and started to yell and scream profanities at his mother and office staff. Most disturbing, on returning home, still upset, he chased the family pet with a pair of scissors. His mother had to run him down and physically remove the scissors from his hands. He needed to be physically restrained and finally calmed down after an hour of physical restraint and consoling.

The family had been referred for counseling by Timothy's pediatrician to address his behaviors when he was four years old. His parents reported that counseling focused on parenting skills and attachment issues stemming from the mother's postpartum depression and the father's extended absence because of job-related assignments. The parents, after six months of counseling and little change in Timothy's behavior, went back to the doctor for another referral. The doctor felt that his impulsive and hyperactive behaviors were "probably" suggestive of ADHD and he would try Timothy on an ADHD medication. His behavior did not improve and actually became worse. He was quickly taken off of the stimulant medication and not put on another medication until the middle of his first-grade year. The parents were skeptical about medication after this experience and, against the advice of his pediatrician, refused to look at another medication. They decided to wait and see before trying medication again.

Timothy had great difficulty in kindergarten. After a number of calls home, aggressive actions toward staff and peers, Timothy's parents voluntarily took him out of school. His mother stayed home to take care of him and home-schooled him with material recommended by the kindergarten teacher. His violent, aggressive, and noncompliant behaviors continued at home, but feeling very discouraged and depressed, the parents did not ask for a mental health evaluation. It is not uncommon for parents of affected children to develop a sense of "learned helplessness": "No matter what I do, nothing works." Typically in such cases, the parent neither rewards good behavior nor addresses the child's problem behaviors. The parents can develop a state of mind where they feel paralyzed and unable to make positive changes in their child's behavior.

Things did not change for Timothy in the first grade. As with his previous school experience, he continued to show significant mood swings, ADHD symptoms, noncompliance, and oppositional behaviors. The final incident that led to Timothy's referral to a mental health specialist was his striking another child over the head with a large toy he had in his backpack. Desperate not to have him kicked out of school, the parents finally agreed to have him evaluated by a child psychiatrist. After a thorough evaluation, Timothy was diagnosed with both ADHD and bipolar disorder. He was placed on a mood-stabilizing medication to first address his bipolar symptoms, and once his mood was stabilized, the psychiatrist placed him on medication for ADHD.

Even with his new medication regimen, however, Timothy was unable to stay in a general-education classroom and was soon placed in a more restrictive educational placement—a classroom for emotionally disturbed children. He is now in the third grade and is still unable to be placed in general education.

Timothy has required psychiatric hospitalization on two occasions because of his behaviors and continues to present significant difficulties at school. His prognosis is difficult to predict.

Reflection

Andy is a child with a clear ADHD diagnosis along with an identified learning disability in written language. When out of control, Andy was experiencing in many ways what Daniel Goleman (1995) called, an "emotional hijacking," in which the emotional part of the brain, the limbic system, declares an emergency, recruiting the rest of the brain to its agenda. The reaction occurs in an instant before the "thinking brain," the neocortex, has a chance to evaluate the situation. Afterward, Andy would have no sense of what came over him, which is the classic hallmark of an emotional hijacking (Goleman, 1995, pp. 13–14). Andy has benefited from medication that should temper his impulsivity, acting out, and inattentive behaviors, but will not address his learning disability. Academic interventions, not medication, address learning disabilities. Medication, however, should help him be more receptive to teacher directions, which in turn should help his academic performance.

Timothy is a young child whose diagnosis of ADHD and bipolar disorder significantly challenge him. Timothy's diagnosis and behaviors are an exception and not the rule for children with ADHD who, for the most part, can be educated in the general-education classroom with only minimal to moderate accommodations to find success.

Resource B

Other Disorders Sometimes Associated With ADHD

ADHD is a disorder that presents uniquely in each affected child. Some children will present with what some professionals refer to as "clean ADHD"—that is, ADHD without associated disorders (also referred to as "comorbid disorders"), but the majority of children referred for psychiatric evaluation have ADHD complicated by comorbidity. These associated disorders tend to adversely influence the child's academic, social, and emotional development. We will be reviewing four comorbid-disorder areas sometimes seen in the ADHD population:

1. Oppositional Defiant Disorder (ODD) and Conduct Disorder (CD)

2. Anxiety Disorders

3. Mood Disorders

4. Bipolar Disorder

Even though there are other disorders associated with ADHD not noted in this list, such as Tourette's syndrome, we have limited our discussion to these five because we have found them to be particularly problematic with respect to behavior and academic performance in children with ADHD. We briefly overview anxiety, mood, and bipolar disorders with a more in-depth discussion of ODD.

You will find an in-depth discussion and overview of learning disabilities in Chapter 5.

ODD

Recent research suggests that approximately 2% to 16% of the general population has ODD. Up to 50% to 60% of children with ADHD, especially those with strong hyperactive and impulsive behaviors (Bloomquist, 1996), are often noncompliant and oppositional. Most children develop ODD prior to the age of 8 years (*DSM-IV-TR*, 2000). Up to 70% of children with ADHD referred to clinics are diagnosed with ODD (Barkley, 1995).

Children with ODD display oppositional and defiant behaviors that are more severe and of a greater magnitude than their same-age peers. These children frequently lose their temper, swear, are often angry or resentful, and appear to be easily annoyed by others. They tend to be extremely stubborn and rarely accept blame for their negative behaviors or mistakes. Some children with ODD can go on to develop a CD, which presents a serious pattern of antisocial behavior and violation of the rights of others. They often bully or intimidate others, can be physically cruel to people and animals, and lie or break promises to get what they want. They may also steal, run away from home, skip school, deliberately destroy others' property, and set fires (*DSM-IV-TR*, 2000). However, a CD is rarely diagnosed in children younger than the ages of five or six years (Campbell, 2002).

The longer the ODD and CD behaviors persist, the more difficult they are to eliminate. Consequently, both the parents and school need to quickly address these behaviors as soon as they are noted. Early intervention is important because it appears that genetic factors, such as those associated with ADHD, "operate as a vulnerability for the possible expression of aggressive conduct problems, but that environmental risk factors and stressors increase the likelihood of expression of these problems" (Bloomquist, 1996, pp. 37–38). By minimizing environmental stressors in an affected child's day, teachers and parents can often temper the possibility of a child developing conditions such as ODD and CD.

Children with ODD and CD are at risk for developing low self-esteem, for being expelled from school, for isolating themselves from peers, and for being drawn to other children with similar challenges.

While various medications can be effective in extreme cases to decrease the severity of ODD and CD, medication alone will not completely eliminate core behaviors related to ODD or CD. These programs are addressed primarily through behavior management programs at home and school, and for some children, through psychotherapy to improve anger management and problem-solving skills.

ADHD does not directly cause ODD and CD, but the presence of ADHD greatly increases the risk for developing ODD and CD. Unfortunately, because affected children tend to attribute both failure and success to external factors, they are less receptive to compliments and often see themselves as victims. They can become defensive and less open to interventions designed to minimize problematic behaviors.

In conclusion, it is common for preschool children to be oppositional at times, and great caution should be used in putting this diagnosis on very young children.

ANXIETY AND MOOD DISORDERS

Anxiety Disorder

Anxiety disorders can manifest a broad range of signs and symptoms and stem from a number of causes. When problematic, younger children tend to fear monsters and ghosts and separation from caretakers. They may be selectively mute, clingy, and sometimes aggressive. Older children usually focus on possible natural disasters or personal and family concerns, or have home and school-related worries. Secondary anxiety disorder is reported to be present in 34% of the ADHD population (August, Realmuto, MacDonald, Nugent, & Crosby, 1996).

Separation Anxiety

Separation anxiety is the only anxiety disorder that is specific to childhood. It manifests itself as "developmentally inappropriate and excessive anxiety concerning separation from home" and "recurrent excessive distress" (*DSM-IV-TR*, 2000, p. 113) about separation from home or major attachment figures.

Like any childhood disorder, the disturbance needs to cause significant distress or impairment in functioning to meet the criteria for the label of "separation anxiety disorder." In most cases, separation anxiety in young children is triggered by a life stress such as a death of a pet, moving to a new home, or a major illness in the family. Campbell (2002) suggests that for young children, their reaction to life stresses may be appropriate considering their age and development. However, she goes on to comment that for some young children, the diagnosis is appropriate.

Mood Disorder

Studies find that children with ADHD and a diagnosis of ODD and CD show higher rates of depression and anxiety, 30% and 34%, respectively (August et al., 1996). Children with ADHD with a diagnosis of Predominantly Inattentive type (ADHD-I) are at more risk for depression than are those children with a Combined classification (ADHD-C; Anastopoulos & Shelton, 2001).

Signs and symptoms of a mood disorder, like depression, often present themselves differently in children compared to adults. Children typically display severe irritability, defiance, underachievement in school, and an exacerbation of their underlying ADHD features.

ADHD children often experience less academic success in school, and they often receive more negative feedback and disciplinary consequences than do unaffected children. An affected child's difficult traits, such as lacking perseverance in the face of failure, poor behavior inhibition that makes it hard for them to pause and think, and difficulty regulating their ongoing emotional reactions, puts them at risk for negative feedback (Barkley, 1997; Weiss & Hechtman, 1993). These factors contribute to the development of anxiety and depressive disorders in some children with ADHD.

Bipolar Disorder

There is a tremendous overlap of symptoms in children with severe ADHD and in those children with bipolar disorder (BD, or manic depression). It is not uncommon for children to be initially diagnosed with ADHD and later with BD, but diagnosing a child with severe ADHD and possible BD is often difficult. In fact, because the symptoms of these disorders overlap so much, a child can sometimes meet the criteria for both diagnoses.

Children may show some of the same symptoms as adults diagnosed with BD; however, younger children commonly display a mixed state, presenting with symptoms of mania and depression: uncharacteristic behaviors of extreme enthusiasm, irritability, and anger. A child with manic symptoms is sometimes referred to as having "bad ADHD" because the most common disturbance in manic children is irritability and *affective storms*, with prolonged and aggressive outbursts. Because the symptoms of irritability can vary in degree and result from a number of causes, the disorder can be mistaken for depression, a CD, or ADHD, so a BD diagnosis may often be missed. In the diagnosis of BD, the involvement of a psychiatrist is important, because for purposes of treatment, medicating for BD is usually different than for ADHD and may be quite complicated.

In conclusion, when working with very young children, clinicians recommend great caution in diagnosing preschool and early school-age children with BD. Recently, however, more children are being diagnosed with BD, and you are likely to be working with some children who will at some time be diagnosed with BD.

Resource C

*Childhood Disorders and
Conditions That Can Mimic
ADHD in Young Children*

The disorders and conditions here have been found to mimic ADHD and are sometimes mistaken for ADHD.

- Unidentified learning disability
- Reactive attachment disorder
- Child abuse (sexual, physical, mental)
- Adjustment disorder (home or school changes)
- Depression
- Bipolar disorder
- Tourette's syndrome
- Regulatory disorder
- Pervasive developmental disorder
- Fragile X syndrome
- Anxiety disorder
- Oppositional defiant disorder
- Separation anxiety disorder
- Mild seizure disorder
- Language-based disorder
- Sensory deficits
- Sensory integration dysfunction
- Mild cerebral palsy
- Malnourishment or sleep-deprivation (including sleep apnea)
- Reaction to medication
- Hyperthyroidism
- Pinworm infection
- Bad fit with the environment (temperament)
- Post-traumatic stress disorder

Resource D

Recommended Books for Teachers

1.2.3. Magic, Effective Discipline for Children (Ages) 2–12, Phelan, T., Ph.D. (1996). Glen Ellyn, IL: Child Management, Inc.

ADAPT: Attention Deficit Accommodations Plan for Teaching. (1991). Plantation, FL: Specialty Press; telephone (ADD Warehouse) (800) 233-9273.

ADD Hyperactivity Workbook for Parents, Teachers, and Kids (2nd ed.). Plantation, FL: Specialty Press; telephone (ADD Warehouse) (800) 233-9273.

ADHD: A Survival Guide for Parents and Teachers, Lougy, R. A., & Rosenthal, D. K. (2002). Duarte, CA: Hope Press.

A Mind at a Time, Levine, M. (2002). New York: Simon and Schuster Publishing.

Attention Deficit Disorder: A Different Perception, Hartmann, T. (1996). Grass Valley, CA: Underwood Books.

Attention Deficit Disorder and Learning Disabilities: Realities, Myths, and Controversial Treatments, Ingersoll, B., & Goldstein, M. (1993). New York: Doubleday.

Attention Deficit Disorders Intervention Manual, McCarney, S. B., Ed.D. (1989). Columbia, MO: Hawthorne Press.

CHADD Educators Manual, Fowler, M. C. (1992). Plantation, FL: CASET Associates.

Children and Disabilities, Barshaw, M. (2002). Baltimore, MD: Brookes Publishing.

Difficult Behavior in Early Childhood: Positive Discipline for PreK–3 Classrooms and Beyond, Mah, R. (2007). Thousand Oaks, CA: Corwin Press.

Helping Your Hyperactive/Attention Deficit Child, Taylor, J., Ph.D. (1994). Rocklin, CA: Prima Publishing.

How to Reach and Teach ADD/ADHD Children, Rief, S. F. (1993). New York: The Center for Applied Research and Education.

I Can't Sit Still: Educating and Affirming Inattentive and Hyperactive Children. (1992). Santa Cruz, CA: ETR Associates.

I'm Somebody Too, Gehret, J. (1992). De Witt, NY: GSI (for children to read).

It's So Much Work to Be Your Friend: Helping the Child With Learning Disabilities Find Social Success, Lavoie, R. (2005). New York: Touchstone Press.

Jumpin' Johnny Get Back to Work! A Guide's Guide to ADHD/Hyperactivity, Gordon, M. (1992). De Witt, NY: GSI (for children to read).

Learning to Slow Down and Pay Attention, Dixon, E., & Nadeau, K. (1991). Chesapeake Psychological Services (for children to read).

Otto Learns About His Medicine: A Story About Medication for Children (Rev. ed.), Galvin, M., Ph.D. (1995). New York: Magination Press (for children to read).

Putting on the Brakes: Young Peoples' Guide to Understanding Attention Deficit Hyperactivity Disorder, Quinn, P., & Stern, J. (1991). New York: Magination Press.

Setting Limits, How to Raise Responsible Independent Children Providing Reasonable Boundaries, MacKenzie, R., Ed.D. (1993). Rocklin, CA: Prima Publishing.

Taking Charge of ADHD: A Complete, Authoritative Guide for Parents, Barkley, R. A., Ph.D. (1995). New York/London: The Guilford Press.

Young Children With Special Needs, Hooper, S. R., & Umansky, W. (2004). Upper Saddle River, NJ: Pearson Education, Inc.

Resource E

Useful Web Sites

All Kinds of Minds
http://www.allkindsofminds.org
This Web site offers an online newsletter to support learning disabilities. The site is a great resource for information on characteristics of students with learning disabilities.

Behavior Management
http://www.disciplinehelp.com

CEC Division for Early Childhood
http://www.dec-sped.org
This is a division of the Council for Exceptional Children, which advocates for individuals who work with and on behalf of children with special needs from birth through age eight and their families.

Center on the Social and Emotional Foundations for Early Learning
http://csefel.uiuc.edu/
The Center on the Social and Emotional Foundations for Early Learning is a national center focused on strengthening the capacity of childcare and Head Start programs to improve the social and emotional outcomes of young children. Training resources are available to download in both English and Spanish.

CHADD: Children and Adults With Attention Deficit/Hyperactivity Disorder
http://www.chadd.org
CHADD works to improve the lives of people with ADHD through education, advocacy, and support. The site includes factsheets, legislative information, research studies, and links.

Council for Exceptional Children
http://www.cec.sped.org
The Council for Exceptional Children site is a national resources for educators and parents. The Web site has articles and news along with an extensive store with books for teachers, parents, and students with disabilities.

LD Online: Addressing Behavior in Schools
http://www.ldonline.org/ld_indepth/special_education/quinn_behavior.html

Learning Disability Association
http://www.ldonline.org
This site is a highly informative resource for teachers, parents, and students with learning disabilities. The site contains numerous articles and links to support individuals with learning differences.

Learning Disability Association of America (LDA)
http://www.ldanatl.org
LDA's purpose is to advance the education and general welfare of children who show handicaps of a perceptual, conceptual, or coordinative nature.

National Center for Learning Disabilities
http://www.ncld.org
The National Center for Learning Disabilities' Web site contains sections for parents, advocates, teachers, and individuals with learning disabilities. This is an informative site with information on the latest research and on Response to Intervention models of early intervention.

Positive Approaches to Challenging Behaviors
http://ici2umn.edu.multistate/default.html

Positive Approaches to Challenging Behaviors for Young Children With Disabilities
http://ici2.umn.edu/preschoolbehavior/
The purpose of this Web site is to discuss positive behavioral supports for young children who engage in challenging behaviors. The information on this Web site is intended to help families, caregivers, and service providers.

Positive Behavioral Interventions and Supports
http://www.pbis.org
The Technical Assistance Center on PBIS has been established by the Office of Special Education Program, U.S. Department of Education, to give

schools capacity-building information and technical assistance for identifying, adapting, and sustaining effective, schoolwide disciplinary practices. The center provides information at the level of individual students, schools, and districts that schoolwide positive behavior intervention and supports are feasible and effective.

Positive Discipline
http://positivediscipline.com
Special Education Disabilities and Disorders
http://www.specialeducation.org/definitions.html
Provides a description of various disabilities

Practical Ideas for Addressing Challenging Behaviors
http://www.sopriswets.com/swstore

Special Education Resources on the Internet
http://www.hood.edu/seri/serihome.html
These are helpful sites for all phases of special education.

Teaching Children with Attention Deficit Disorder
http://www.kidsource.com/kidsource/conent2/add.html
This site defines the different types of ADHD and a proper learning environment.

Teaching LD
http://www.teachingld.org
The Division of Learning Disabilities of the Council for Exceptional Children Web site has news and Web features for teachers and parents of individual with learning disabilities.

References

Alessandri, S. M. (1992). Attention, play, and social behavior in ADHD preschoolers. *Journal of Abnormal Child Psychology, 20,* 289–302.

American Academy of Pediatrics. *ADHD-coexisting conditions.* Retrieved April 12, 2006, from http://www.aap.org/pubed/zzz6zrwvysc.htm

American Medical Association's Council of Scientific Affairs. (1998). *Journal of the American Medical Association, 279.*

American Psychiatric Association. (2000). *Diagnostic and statistical manual of mental disorders* (4th ed., text rev.). Washington, DC: Author.

Anastopoulos, A. D., & Shelton, T. L. (2001). *Assessing attention-deficit/hyperactivity disorder.* New York: Kluwer Academic/Plenum.

Arnsten, A. F., Steere, J. C., & Hunt, R. D. (1996). The contribution of alpha2-noradrenergic mechanisms of prefrontal cortical cognitive function: Potential significance for attention-deficit hyperactivity disorder. *Archives of General Psychiatry, 53,* 448–455.

August, G. H., & Garfinkel, G. D. (1990). Comorbidity of ADHD and reading disability among clinic-referred children. *Journal of Abnormal Psychology, 18,* 29–45.

August, G. J., Realmuto, G. M., MacDonald, A. W., III, Nugent, S. M., & Crosby, R. (1996, October). Prevalence of ADHD and comorbid disorders among elementary school children screened for disruptive behavior. *Journal of Abnormal Child Psychology, 24*(5), 571–595.

Auiler, J. F., Liu, K., Lynch, J. M., & Gelotte, C. K. (2002). Effect of food on early drug exposure from extended-release stimulants: Results from the Concerta(A)®, Adderall XRa, food evaluation (CAFA%) study. *Current Medical Research Opinion, 18,* 311–316.

Barkley, R. A. (1990). *Attention-deficit hyperactivity disorder: A handbook for diagnosis and treatment.* New York: Guilford Press.

Barkley, R. A. (1995). *Taking charge of ADHD: The complete authoritative guide for parents.* New York: Guilford Press.

Barkley, R. A. (1997). *ADHD and the nature of self-control.* New York: Guilford Press.

Barkley, R. A. (2000). *Taking charge of ADHD: The complete authoritative guide for parents.* (Rev. ed.) New York: Guilford Press.

Batsche, G., Elliot, J., Graden, J. L., Grimes, J., Kovaleski, J. F., Prasse, D., et al. (2005). *Response to intervention: Policy considerations and implementation.* Washington, DC: National Association of State Directors of Special Education, Inc.

Batshaw, M. (2002). *Children with disabilities.* Baltimore: Brookes.

Biederman, J., Faraone, S. V., Keenan, K., Benjamin, J., Krifcher, B., Moore, C., et al. (1992). Further evidence for family-genetic risk factors in attention-deficit hyperactivity disorder: Patterns of comorbidity in probands and relatives of psychiatrically and pediatrically referred samples. *Archives of General Psychiatry, 49*, 728–738.

Bloomquist, M. L. (1996). *Skills training for children with behavior disorders: A parent and therapist handbook.* New York: Guilford Press.

Breggin, P. R. (1998). *Talking back to Ritalin: What doctors aren't telling you about stimulants for children.* Monroe, ME: Common Courage Press.

Browning Wright, D. (2003, February 20). *Teaching and learning trainings.* Paper presented at the CARS+ Convention, San Jose, NM.

Brunk, D. (2000, February). Federal report spotlights issues in ADHD diagnosis. *Clinical Psychiatry News, 1,* 5.

Bukstein, O. G. (2006). Current opinions and new developments in the pharmacology treatment of ADHD. *Remedica, 1*(1), 8–15.

Burgess, J. R. (1998, September 2–3). *Attention deficit hyperactivity disorder: Observational and interventional studies.* Paper presented at the National Institutes of Health Workshop on Omega-3 Essential Fatty Acids and Psychiatric Disorders, Bethesda, MD.

Campbell, S. B. (2002). *Behavior problems in preschool children: Clinical and developmental issues* (2nd ed.). New York: Guilford Press.

Campbell, S. B., Pierce, E. W., March, C. L., Ewing, L. J., & Szumowski, E. K. (1994). Hard-to-manage preschool boys: Symptomatic behavior across contexts and time: Guide for Professionals. *Child Development, 65,* 836–851.

Canter, L. (1996). First, the rapport—then, the rules. *Learning, 24*(5), 12–14.

Canter, L., & Canter, M. (1993). *Succeeding with difficult students: New strategies for reaching your most challenging students.* Santa Monica, CA: Lee Canter & Associates.

Carey, W. B., & McDevitt, S. C. (1995). *Coping with children's temperament: A guide for professionals.* New York: Basic Books.

Chappell, P. B., Phillip, B., Riddle, M. A., Scahill, L., Lynch, A., Schults, R., et al. (1995, September). Guanfacine treatment of comorbid attention-deficit hyperactivity disorder and Tourette's syndrome: Preliminary clinical experience. *Journal of the American Academy of Child & Adolescent Psychiatry, 34,* 1140–1146.

Charles, C. M. (2005). *Building classroom discipline* (8th ed.). Boston: Allyn & Bacon/Pearson.

Charles, C. M., & Senter, G. W. (2005). *Elementary classroom management* (4th ed.). Boston: Allyn & Bacon/Pearson.

Colquhoun, I., & Bunday, S. (1981). A lack of essential fatty acids as a possible cause of hyperactivity in children. *Medical Hypotheses, 7,* 673–679.

Comings, D. E. (2001). *Tourette syndrome and human behavior.* Duarte, CA: Hope Press.

Conners, C. K., Casat, C. D., Gualtieri, C. T., & Weller, E. M. (1996). Bupropion hydrochloride in attention deficit disorder with hyperactivity. *Journal of the American Academy of Child & Adolescent Psychiatry, 35,* 1314–1321.

Current ADHD insights: A summary of recent presentations on ADHD. (2004, February). Hasbrouck Heights, NJ: MedLearning.

DeGeorge, K. L. (1998). *Using children's literature to teach social skills.* Retrieved June 17, 2005, from http://www.ldonline.org/articles/6194?theme=print

Denham, S. A. (1998). *Emotional development in young children.* New York: Guilford Press.

DeRuvo, S., & DeRuvo, F. (2000). *Report writing: Removing the stress!* Granite Bay, CA: Adroit.

Douglas, V., & Parry, P. A. (1994). Effects of reward and nonreward on frustration attention-deficit disorder. *Journal of Abnormal Child Psychology, 22,* 281–302.

Doyle, A. E. (2006). Executive functions in attention-deficit/hyperactive disorder. *Journal of Clinical Psychiatry, 67*(Suppl. 8), 21–26.

DuPaul, G. J., McGocy, K. E., Eckert, T. L., & Van Brakle, J. (2001). Preschool children with attention-deficit/hyperactivity disorder: Impairments in behavioral, social, and school functioning. *Journal of the American Academy of Child & Adolescent Psychiatry, 40,* 508–515.

Durston, S., Tottenham, N. T., Thomas, K. M., Davidson, I. E., Yihong, Y., Ulug, A. M., et al. (2003). Differential patterns of striatal activation in young children with and without ADHD. *Biological Psychiatry, 53,* 871–878.

Egger, J., Stella, A., & McEwen, L. (1992). Controlled trial of hyposensitification with food-induced hyperkinetic syndrome. *Lancet, 334,* 1150–1153.

Fink-Chorzempka, B., Graham, S., & Harris, K. R. (2005). What can I do to help young children who struggle with writing? *Teaching Exceptional Children, 37,* 64–66.

Firestone, P., Musten, L. M., Pisterman, S., Mercer, J., & Bennett, S. (1998). Short-term side effects of stimulant medication are increased in preschool children with attention-deficit/hyperactivity disorder: A double-blind placebo-controlled study. *Journal of Child & Adolescent Psychopharmacology, 8,* 13–25.

Frick, P. J., & Lahey, B. B. (1991). Nature and characteristics of attention-deficit hyperactivity disorder. *School Psychology Review, 20,* 163–173.

Garber, S., Garber, M., & Spizman, R. (1996). *Beyond Ritalin.* New York: Harper Perennial.

Goldberg Edelson, M. (1995). *Social stories.* Retrieved October 18, 2006, from http://www.autism.org/stories.html

Goldstein, S., & Goldstein, M. (1998). *Managing attention deficit hyperactivity disorders in children: A guide for practioners* (2nd ed.). New York: John Wiley and Sons.

Goleman, D. (1995). *Emotional Intelligence: Why it can matter more than I.Q.* New York: Bantam Books.

Gray Center for Social Learning and Understanding. (2006). *Welcome to the social stories website.* Retrieved on November 1, 2006, from http://www.thegraycenter.org/socialstories.cfm

Gregory, G. H., & Chapman, C. (2007). *Differentiated instructional strategies: One size doesn't fit all* (2nd ed). Thousand Oaks, CA: Corwin Press.

Gustafsson, P., Thernlund, G., Ryding, E., Rosén, I., & Cederblad, M. (2000). Associations between cerebral blood-flow measured by single photon emission computed tomography (SPECT), electro-encephalogram (EEG), behaviour symptoms, cognition and neurological soft signs in children with attention-deficit hyperactivity disorder (ADHD). *Acta Paediatrica, 89*, 830–835.

Hallowell, E., & Ratey, J. (1994). *Driven to distraction: Recognizing and coping with attention deficit disorder from childhood through adult.* New York: Simon and Schuster.

Hoagwood, K., Jensen, P. S., Feil, M., Benedetto, V., & Bhatara, V. S. (2000, October). Medication management of stimulants in pediatric practice settings: A national perspective. *Journal of Developmental and Behavioral Pediatrics, 2*, 322–331.

Hooper, S. R., & Umansky, W. (2004). *Young children with special needs.* Upper Saddle River, NJ: Pearson Education.

Hunt, R. D., Armsten, A. F., & Asbell, M. D. (1995). An open trial of guanfacine in the treatment of attention-deficit hyperactivity disorder. *Journal of the American Academy of Child and Adolescent Psychiatry, 34*, 50–54.

Karpel, M. (1994). *Evaluating couples: Handbook for practitioners.* Scranton, PA: Norton Press.

Kelleher, K. J., McInerny, T. K., & Gardner, W. P. (2000, June). Increasing identification of psychosocial problems: 1979–1996. *Pediatrics, 105*, 1313–1321.

Lavigne, J. V., Gibbons, R. D., Christoffel, K. K., Arend, R., Rosenbaum, D., Binns, H., et al. (1996). Prevalence rates and correlates of psychiatric disorders among preschool children. *Journal of the American Academy of Child and Adolescent Psychiatry, 35*, 204–214.

Lavoie, R. (1996a). *Learning disabilities and discipline with Richard Lavoie: When the chips are down. . . . Strategies for improving children's behavior, a program guide.* Washington, DC: Learning Disabilities Project at WETA.

Lavoie, R. (1996b). *When the chips are down. . . . Strategies for improving children's behavior* [Videocassette]. Washington, DC: Learning Disabilities Project at WETA.

Lavoie, R. (2005). *It's so much work to be your friend: Helping the child with learning disabilities find social success.* New York: Touchstone Press.

Layey, B. B., Pelham, W. E., Stein, M. A., Loney, J., Trapani, C., Nugent, K., et al. (1998). Validity of *DSM-IV* attention-deficit/hyperactivity disorder for younger children. *Journal of the American Academy of Child and Adolescent Psychiatry, 37*, 695–701.

Levine, M. (1987). Attention deficits: The diverse effects of weak control systems in childhood. *Pediatric Annals, 16*, 117–130.

Levine, M. (2002). *A mind at a time.* New York: Simon & Schuster.

Levine, M., Busch, B., & Aufesser, C. (1982). The dimension of inattention in children with school problems. *Pediatrics, 70*, 387.

Levy, F., Hay, D. A., McStephen, M., Wood, C., & Waldman, I. (1997). Attention-deficit hyperactivity disorder: A category or a continuum? Genetic analysis of a large-scale twin study. *Journal of the American Academy of Child and Adolescent Psychiatry, 36*, 737–744.

Lougy, R. A., & Rosenthal, D. K. (2002). *ADHD: A survival guide for parents and teachers.* Duarte, CA: Hope Press.

Mariani, M., & Barkley, R. A. (1997). Neuropsychological and academic functioning in preschool children with attention-deficit hyperactivity disorder. *Developmental Neuropsychology, 13*, 111–129.

Marshall, R. M., Schafer, V. A., O'Donnell, L., Elliot, J., & Hardwick, M. L. (1999). Arithmetic disabilities and ADD subtypes: Implications for *DSM-IV*. *Journal of Learning Disabilities, 32*, 240.

Mayer-Johnson. (n.d.). Homepage. Retrieved November 1, 2006, from http://www.mayerjohnson.com

McGee, R., Williams, S., & Freeman, M. (1992). Attention deficit disorder and age of onset of problem behaviors. *Journal of Abnormal Child Psychology, 20*, 487–502.

McIntosh, D. E., & Cole-Love, A. S. (1996). Profile comparison between ADHD and non-ADHD children on the Temperament Assessment Battery for Children. *Journal of Psychoeducational Assessment, 14*, 362–372.

Michigan ranks third in nation in prescribing Ritalin: Some say schools turn to medication to control students. Ritalin's routine use raises alarm over diagnosis, goals. Use of Ritalin in schools nearly out of control. (1998, March 8). *Detroit News*.

Minde, K. (1998). The use of psychotropic medication in preschoolers: Some recent developments. *Canadian Journal of Psychiatry, 43*, 571–575.

Mitchell, E. A., Aman, M. G., Turbott, S. H., & Manku, M. (1987). Clinical characteristics and serum essential fatty acid levels in hyperactive children. *Clinical Pediatrics, 26*, 406–411.

Nakamura, R. (2002, September 26). *Testimony before the Committee on Government Reform*. U.S. House of Representatives OLPA Hearings, 107th Congress.

National Institute of Mental Health. (1999, December 14). *Questions & answers*. Author.

Pelham, W. E., & Fabiano, G. (2001). *Behavioral modification. Child and Adolescent Psychiatric Clinics of North America, 9*, 671–688.

Pfiffner, L. J., & Barkley, R. A. (1990). Educational placement and classroom management. In R. A. Barkley (Ed.), *Attention deficit hyperactivity disorder: A handbook for diagnosis and treatment* (pp. 498–539). New York: Guilford Press.

Pisterman, S., McGrath, P., Firestone, P., et al. (1989). Outcome of parent-mediated treatment of preschoolers with attention deficit disorder with hyperactivity. *Journal of Consulting and Clinical Psychology, 57*, 628–635.

Porter, L. (2002). *Educating children with special needs*. Thousand Oaks, CA: Sage.

Quinn, P. O. (1997). *Attention deficit disorder: Diagnosis and treatment from infancy to adulthood*. New York: Brunner/Mazel.

Rappley, M. D., Mullan, P. B., Alvarez, F. J., Eneli, I. U., Wang, J., & Gardiner, J. C. (1999). Diagnosis of attention-deficit/hyperactivity disorder and use of psychotropic medication in very young children. *Archives of Pediatrics and Adolescent Medicine, 153*, 1039–1045.

Rief, S. R. (1998). *The ADD/ADHD checklist: An easy reference for parents and teachers*. San Francisco: Jossey-Bass.

Rief, S. R. (2005). *How to reach and teach children with ADD/AD: Practical techniques, strategies and intervention*. San Francisco: Jossey-Bass.

Rothenberg, S. (2005). *Playing with self-esteem: The importance of social skills*. Retrieved October 18, 2006, from http://members.bellatlantic.net/~pshrync/play.html

Ruiz, N. (1997). *Optimal learning environments for bilingual special education students*. Fresno, CA: California State University.

Scahill, L., Chappell, P. B., Young, S. K., Schultz, R. T., Katsovich, L., Shepherd, E., et al. (2001, July). A placebo-controlled study of guanfacine in the treatment of children with tic disorders and attention deficit hyperactivity disorder. *American Journal of Psychiatry, 158,* 1067–1074.

Scahill, L., & Schwab Stone, M. (2000). Epidemiology of ADHD in school-age children. *Child and Adolescent Psychiatry Clinics of North America, 9,* 541–555.

Schetter, P. (2004). *Learning the R.O.P.E.S. for improved executive function.* Woodland, CA: Autism & Behavior Associates.

Shekim, W. O., Javid, J., Dans, J. M., & Bylund, D. B. (1983). Effects of D-amphetamine on urinary metabolites on dopamine and norepinephrine in hyperactive children. *Biological Psychiatry, 18,* 707–714.

Short, E J., Manos, M. J., Findling R. L., & Schubel, E. A. (2004). A prospective study of stimulant response in preschool children: Insights from ROC analyses. *Journal of the American Academy of Child and Adolescent Psychiatry, 43,* 251–259.

Siegel, D. J. (1999). *The developing mind: How relationships and the brain interact to shape who we are.* New York: Guilford Press.

Smutney, J. F., & von Fremd, S. E. (2004). *Differentiating for the young child: Teaching across the content areas (K-3).* Thousand Oaks, CA: Corwin Press.

Taylor, J. (1994). *Helping your hyperactive attention deficit child.* Rocklin, CA: Prima.

Teeter, P. A. (1998). *Interventions for ADHD: Treatment in developmental context.* New York: Guilford Press.

Thomas, A., Chess, S., Birch, H. G., Hertiz, M. E., & Korn, S. (1963). *Behavioral individuality in early childhood.* New York: New York University Press.

Tomlinson, C. A. (2000, August). *Differentiation of instruction in the elementary grades.* Retrieved on July 25, 2006, from ERIC Clearinghouse on Elementary and Early Childhood Education at http://ceep.crc.uiuc.edu/eecearchive/digests/2000/tomlin00.pdf

Tomlinson, C. A. (2001). *How to differentiate instruction in mixed-ability classrooms* (2nd ed.). Alexandria, VA: Association for Supervision and Curriculum Development.

Vaidya, C. J., Austin, G., Kirkorian, G., Ridlehuber, H. W., Desmond, J. E., Glover, G. H., et al. (1998). Selective effects of methylphenidate in attention deficit hyperactivity disorder: A functional magnetic resonance study. *Proceedings of the National Academy of Sciences, 95,* 14494–14499.

Vaughan, B. S., & Kratochvil, C. J. (2006). Pharmacotherapy of ADHD in young children. *Psychiatry, 3*(8), 36–45.

Walker, J. E., Shea, T. M., & Bauer, A. M. (2004). *Behavior management: A practical approach for educators.* Upper Saddle River, NJ: Pearson Education, Inc.

Weiss, G., & Hechtman, L. T. (1993). *Hyperactive children grown up: ADHD in children, adolescents, and adults* (2nd ed.). New York: Guilford Press.

Wiggins, G., & McTighe, J. (1998). *Understanding by design.* Alexandria, VA: Association for Supervision and Curriculum Development.

Wolraich, M., Wilson, D. B., & White, J. W. (1995). The effect of sugar on behavior or cognition in children: A meta-analysis. *Journal of the American Medical Association, 274,* 1617–1621.

Wong, H. K., & Wong, R. T. (2001). *How to be an effective teacher: The first days of school.* Mountain View, CA: Harry K. Wong.

Zentell, S. S., & Dywer, A. M. (1988). Color effects on the impulsivity and activity of hyperactive children. *Journal of School Psychology, 23,* 83–89.

Zito, J. M., Safer, D. J., dosReis, S., Gardner, J. F., Boles, C., & Frances, L. (2000). Trends in the prescribing of psychotropic medications to preschoolers. *Journal of the American Medical Association, 283,* 1025–1030.

Zuvekas, S. H., Vitiello, B., & Norquist, G. S. (2006, April). Recent trends in stimulant medication use among U.S. children. *American Journal of Psychiatry, 163,* 579–585.

Index

CORWIN PRESS

The Corwin Press logo—a raven striding across an open book—represents the union of courage and learning. Corwin Press is committed to improving education for all learners by publishing books and other professional development resources for those serving the field of PreK–12 education. By providing practical, hands-on materials, Corwin Press continues to carry out the promise of its motto: **"Helping Educators Do Their Work Better."**